When Destiny Calls

H·J OTTEWELL

Ordering Information:

Prime Seven Media
518 Landmann St.
Tomah City, WI 54660

Printed in the United States of America

Table of Contents

Chapter 1 1
Chapter 2 8
Chapter 3 15
Chapter 4 23
Chapter 5 29
Chapter 6 34
Chapter 7 40
Chapter 8 47
Chapter 9 55
Chapter 10 62
Chapter 11 68
Chapter 12 74
Chapter 13 79
Chapter 14 84
Chapter 15 90
Chapter 16 95
Chapter 17 101
Chapter 18 107
Chapter 19 117
Chapter 20 124
Chapter 21 128
Chapter 22 137
Chapter 23 144
Chapter 24 149
Chapter 25 160
Chapter 26 167
Chapter 27 172
Chapter 28 183

Chapter 29...191
Chapter 30...198
Chapter 31 210
Chapter 32...219
Chapter 33...226
Chapter 34...235
Chapter 35...242

Chapter 1

Annie was daydreaming again as she crossed the busy London street. Her mind was amid the peace and tranquillity of bye-gone days. She was not aware of the approaching danger as she stepped in front of the oncoming car. The driver had no where to go, he couldn't avoid hitting her.

"Quick, someone, phone for an ambulance," shouted a distraught woman in the crowd of people that had gathered around, seemingly out of no where and they had brought the bust London traffic to a grinding halt. The ambulance arrived in a matter of minutes with its siren screaming.

"Is she alive?" asked some one in the crowd.

"She is still with us, but only just," replied the paramedic as they placed her swiftly but gently into the back of the ambulance and sped away in the direction of the hospital. It was two days later when Annie regained consciousness.

"Where am I?" "What happened?" she asked the nurse who was hovering over her.

"You were knocked over by a car and you are in hospital," replied the nurse in a soothing voice.

"Now, my love, are you able to tell me your name and where you live?" she asked.

"My name is Ann Louise Barnett, but every one just call me Annie," she replied.

"As for my home, that went years ago," she said and a silent tear slipped down her pale, bruised face, as she swiftly recalled the dreadful set of circumstances that had brought her to where she was today.

"All right, Annie, try and get some sleep now," said the nurse as she slipped out of the room and into the corridor leading to the next patient. Her heart went out to the poor, frail old lady who had looked so ragged and dirty when she had been admitted, but who spoke with such a genteel and educated voice. What secrets lay behind those tired but beautiful blue eyes? She wondered.

Annie lay back into the pillows, closed her eyes and found herself slipping back in time to when she was just seven years old. It was her birthday and her beloved Papa had bought her, her very own pony. It was a beautiful little bay mare. She could still feel the excitement of the first time she sat on Starlight's back. How she had loved that little pony and she remembered all of the happy hours they had spent riding around Papa's country estate. This to a child's eyes had seemed enormous.

It was just on the turn of the 19th century and life for the landed gentry was good. She had lived in a beautiful country mansion with formal laid out gardens, very colourful informal gardens, the obligatory kitchen garden and acres of woodland. There were many special places for her and her brother Marcus to hide and play in.

Of course there were many household servants plus a Nanny, and gardeners and one of the gardener's boys also doubled up as a groom for Starlight. They were all treated very well and even with respect for the work which they did. All of the household staff had their own rooms at the top of the house because many of them had come from miles away to get employment at the mansion. The gardeners however went home to their wives and families when their day's work was done, because they lived locally in the nearest village.

Life for Annie and Marcus was idyllic.

Her memories faded for a while as she was awakened by some one touching her arm. It was the doctor who wanted to examine her poor battered body.

"I'm sorry to have awakened you," he said. "My name is Doctor Howard and I shall be caring for you while you are here." "How are you feeling today?" "Are you in much pain?" he asked.

"I hurt all over," she said as she tried to move, but the pain inside was unbearable.

"I'll ask the nurse to give you something for the pain," he said, as he softly touched her hand and left the room.

The nurse arrived shortly afterwards and gave her an injection and she drifted off to sleep again, still feeling the gentle touch of the Doctors hand on hers. As she drifted into sleep state she was aware of holding tightly onto some one else's hand. It was her darling Jamie leading her onto the dance floor at her engagement party. Papa and Mamma stood side by side, looking proudly on as their dearest daughter floated around the ballroom floor with her, soon to be, fiancé. How well suited they were. He was tall and slim and very handsome in his cavalry officers uniform and she, with flowing black curls and trim svelte like figure looked like an angel in a cloud of midnight blue satin. His arm easily encompassed her tiny waist as he danced her across the floor towards the balcony outside which overlooked the Lilly pond. He wanted her to himself at this moment, away from all of the crowd and prying eyes inside the house. Once outside he dropped to one knee as he asked her to share the rest of her life with him. She slowly leaned forward and stroked his handsome face as she whispered, "Yes." He then slipped a stunning ruby ring onto the third finger of her left hand and then they shared a long, lingering embrace. Then his lips burning with desire met hers in a passionate kiss that held all the promise of a life time that she longed for. She wished and hoped that the feelings of love and joy that they felt at this moment could last forever. She felt is if they were the only two people in the world and what a magnificent world it was.

"How is our patient doing today nurse?" asked Doctor Howard as he entered Annie's room

She shook her head. "There's not much response from her," she said "Just continue to do every thing that you can to make her comfortable," said the Doctor

Annie was only vaguely aware of what was being said as she drifted out of consciousness again but how clearly she recalled those distant memories.

She recalled that dreadful day when Jamie had told her that he and his regiment were going overseas and that her brother, Marcus had also joined the army. It was 1914 and the country was at war. She was totally distraught.

There were only two months to go before their wedding.

Mamma had tried her best to console her, but there was nothing that she could say or do to ease the pain that her darling daughter was feeling so Mamma took charge and cancelled all of the wedding arrangements. Dear Mamma, she was a tower of strength, Annie didn't know how she would have managed without her wonderful Mamma taking charge and doing all of the things that she knew she should have been doing, but she just couldn't face up to anything at the moment.

The months past slowly as she waited for news from Jamie, but none arrived. Instead there was a telegram saying that he had been one of the first fatalities of the war. The telegram fell from her hand as she slowly walked up the stairs and went into her room. She was numb all over, too numb to even cry. She lay on her bed and stared up at the ceiling. She didn't know how long she had lain there. Was it hours or was it days? Did it really matter? Her beloved Jamie would not be coming back to her. Time and time again Mamma came and knocked at her door but she made no response. Annie didn't want to hear her, didn't want to speak to her or any one. What was the use of living without her darling Jamie coming home to be at her side?

The moon rose and fell without her even noticing it on that first night, but as it rose on the second night she felt compelled to go to the window to look at it. It was as if Jamie was calling to her from above. She couldn't explain what she was feeling but just knew in her heart that this is what he would want her to do. As she stared at the night sky she remembered what he had said to her before he left to go overseas. She remembered his warm breath on her face as he whispered in her ear, that when the moon was high in the sky they would both look up at it and think of each other, then nothing on this earth could ever keep them apart. The love which they carried for each other would last an eternity.

It was as she looked up to the sky and thought of what might have been that the first tear drop fell and then she just gave in and cried uncontrollably. As the tears fell she felt a strange kind of release. Her mind, her thoughts were beginning to function again. She knew that the love that she held for Jamie would never die, but perhaps now she could face the future and try to rebuild her life. She thought how lucky she was. She still had a loving family and there was still Marcus to think about. She slowly gathered her thoughts together, washed, changed her clothes and prepared herself to go down stairs to face her parents and the future alone.

It was six months later that news came of Marcus's imminent arrival. He had suffered a serious leg wound but was now well enough to make the long journey home. He was being discharged because of the injury he sustained in battle. The war, for him, was now over. How Mamma cried with tears of joy as she read his letter. Papa too, seemed to have a trace of tears in his eyes as he listened to his wife read the letter for the second time.

Annie was at last able to put aside her heartache as she helped with the preparations for her brother's arrival. If only both the men in her life were coming home together she thought to herself.

Marcus arrived two days later looking pale and drawn.

Papa helped him into the sitting room where Mamma and Annie were waiting. Mamma hugged him and told him how much they had all missed him and how wonderful it was to have him back. Mamma chatted on for quite some time telling him all about everything that had happened on the estate while he had been away. And of course every one wanted to know what had happened to him while he had been away from them, but he wasn't interested in talking or hearing about such mundane matters. He had other things on his mind to think about.

Everything about him had changed he was not the fun loving young man that had left home only a year earlier. Instead he appeared to be very surly and aggressive. No one could believe that the man who sat in front of them now, could ever have been, that wonderful, caring and sensitive boy of just one year ago.

Chapter 2

Annie drifted slowly back to consciousness to the sound of some one gently calling her name. She slowly opened her eyes to see the blurred face of the nurse at the side of her bed. "Annie, can you hear me?" the nurse was asking.

Annie managed a weak smile before she drifted off again. Her thoughts went straight back to Marcus. He had been at home for about two years now. Papa had been dead for about 18 months. He had suffered a sudden heart attack while out riding alone. By the time he had been found it was too late for any one to help him.

After Papa's death Marcus took over the running of the family home and estate and he had become a tyrant. Most of the servants had left their employ because of the obnoxious way in which he treated them all. This meant that Annie now had to do most of the household chores because there was no one who wanted to work for the family any more. Cook was the only one who was still with them but Annie was afraid that even she wouldn't take much more of the abuse that Marcus levelled at her.

How her life had changed. No longer was she the carefree young woman of yesteryear. Instead she was now, no more than a drudge, a virtual slave being dictated to, by a stranger in her own home. Poor Mamma had taken to her bed and taken to drinking. Most of the time, she was oblivious of what was happening around her. And as each day passed she was getting weaker and weaker because of the lack of food that she ate. Annie would painstakingly make her favourite meals in the hope to encourage her to eat but without any success. How could this dreadful thing have happened to them Annie wondered to herself. What sort of future do we face? She prayed every day for their situation to improve but instead of that they became steadily worse. Mamma died from the effects of the drink and a broken heart and Annie felt totally isolated and alone. Now she had absolutely no one that she could turn to for help when Marcus was in one of his terrible rages. Now she would have to stand up to him alone the thought terrified her. Shortly after Mamma's death cook finally handed in her notice and left almost immediately. Total and utter despair overwhelmed Annie, how was she expected to cope with all the demands that her brother made on her.

She tried very hard to explain to Marcus that he would have to change his attitude and that he must employ new staff for the household to run properly. But he was not interested in her whining and he informed her that now would be a good time for her to learn how to cook. He also informed her that he expected his meals to be on the table when ever he wished to eat and to add insult to injury he informed her that in future she could eat her meals in the kitchen. He didn't want to have to look at her dirty, disarrayed appearance when he sat down to eat. This felt to her like the ultimate insult.

The situation gradually went from bad to worse when she discovered that Marcus had taken to gambling. He would be up all night playing cards with friends at home, expecting her to wait on them or if not at home he was at one of their houses. He was losing thousands of pounds on a gamble, but had very little to give to his sister for the every day expenses incurred running a house and feeding them both. On one occasion when she had tried to talk rationally to him about their problem he struck her. She was absolutely stunned with disbelief at his actions. She looked into his eyes and saw nothing, no remorse, no pity for her. He just cursed her for troubling him about things which did not concern her. Annie sobbed as she wondered what on earth would become of them.

What had happened to Marcus during those months in 1914 to change him into the monster that he had now, become. And again she wondered how long their present situation could continue. But she still had one place where she could escape from her nightmare. She could still let her thoughts wander to her beloved Jamie and she could dream of the life that could have been hers away from this dreadful house and Marcus. She hated everything about her life and herself, because she hadn't the strength to stand up and fight this worsening situation.

She could only stand by and watch as the contents of the house began disappearing. At first it was just one or two little valuable items, the silver candle sticks, Papa's diamond cufflinks, his, gold watch and chain that went to gambling debts. But the more he played the more he lost and soon paintings and furniture were being sold to pay for his pleasures.

Why couldn't he see how he was destroying every thing around them but even worse than the material objects, he was destroying himself.

Fifteen long lonely years went by with each day being the same as the one before living in fear of what her brother would do next. But not even he could know of the time that she spent contemplating the beauty of the moon and the nearness she felt to her darling Jamie, she felt as though it was these brief moments that gave her courage and kept her sanity in this insane world in which she was trapped.

It was during one of these quiet moments that Annie sat in front of her dressing table mirror contemplating her reflection. She found it hard to recognise the face that peered back at her. She no longer had the flowing curly black locks that used to shine, like a ravens back, her hair truly had been her crowning glory. Now all she saw were lank greying stresses that hung limply from her head.

Gone also was the laughter in her still beautiful, but sad blue eyes. The bloom of youth had also gone forever from her perfect English rose skin and had been replaced by a pale, drawn and lined face. She looked far older than her approaching fortieth year.

Her birthday came and went unnoticed as usual, it was just as any other day, and there was absolutely nothing to celebrate about these days. The days continued to pass into weeks and the weeks into months as they had for many years now, until one day she heard quite a commotion at the door. Who could it be? No-one ever came calling these days. But as she approached the door she heard angry shouting and banging, dare she open it at all she wondered, but the noise would not stop and the voices seemed to be getting angrier with every passing minute. So she took a deep breath and opened the door only to be confronted by many angry tradesmen demanding to speak to her brother.

"I am very sorry," replied Annie. "I don't know where he is or what time he will be back."

"That's not good enough," replied the man nearest to her. "Your brother owes us all money, and we have come here to collect it. If we don't get satisfaction, we will take him to court and then the bailiffs will get what is owing to us," he said in a menacing voice.

"I understand your problem but there is nothing that I can do for you at this precise moment." "If you can wait until my brother comes home, I will try and speak to him then." She promised them.

"Alright Miss," said a man at the back of the group. "We will leave it for the present, but if we don't get our money by Tuesday of next week, then you know what will happen." "We didn't want it to come to this but we all have families to feed and need the money a lot more than your waster of a brother," the man explained. With that they all tipped their hats, turned and left the way they came.

She closed the door, thankful that the confrontation hadn't been any worse, but what could she do about any of it. She dreaded speaking to Marcus about any of it because she never knew how he would react. She already feared for her safety, in fact at times she feared for her life when he was very drunk.

It was shear desperation that forced her to go into Mamma's room, which she had left exactly as it was when Mamma died. She would sell some of her Mamma's jewels, the emerald necklace and ear ring set should fetch a good price she thought. They had been handed down through the family and rightly belonged to Annie, but what does it matter she thought, she would never go anywhere now where she could wear them. How she hated her brother at that moment for forcing her into a position where she contemplated getting rid of the only possessions she had in the world that had belonged to some one she loved dearly. She would never forgive him for that. She reached forward onto the dressing table and picked up the jewel box. That's strange she thought to herself, it had always felt heavier than that. She opened the box and sank to the floor in horror and disbelief. How could he? How could he have done this to her, the box was absolutely empty, he had left nothing for her.

When he arrived home she confronted him with the empty box but he laughed in her face. "What good were they doing, sitting up there?' he asked her completely oblivious of the pain he had caused her. "They were more useful to me." "They gave me a few hours of pleasure, that is, for as long as they lasted," he said with a chilling laugh that sent a shudder down her spine.

What demon had possessed him? He knew how she had treasured those things that Mamma had left her but it meant nothing to him. She now knew that the only thing that was left for him to lose was the very home that they stood in now and that they had both loved so much as children. Her pleas for him to change his ways fell on deaf ears. Even when she told him of the confrontation she had had with the creditors he dismissed her with a booted foot which fortunately she managed to dodge.

True to their word the creditors were again banging on the door demanding payments, but as always her brother was no where to be seen, she had no idea where he went these days. She could not face those angry men again by herself instead she found a dark corner and hid, listening to the bangs and the curses getting louder and louder.

Until finally after what seemed like an eternity it all went quiet but she knew that this was the end of her life in this house. The next callers would be the bailiffs to evict them. How could she face the shame that her brother had brought upon them.

Chapter 3

It was two days later that her brother finally decided to return home in his usual dishevelled and drunken state. She told him what had happened and he fell about laughing at the irony of it all.

"They don't have to worry," he said "It's gone, it's all gone!"

For the first time in years there seemed to be a faint hint of sanity, a faint glimpse of his knowing what he had done to them both. But it was soon gone as he sat at the kitchen table and roared at her to get him some food.

The day that she had dreaded for years had finally arrived, now they hadn't even got a home to call their own. But even in the darkness of her despair, with their present situation, for her, there was at least one glimmer of light now. She would be able to get away from the brother she had come to hate so much, the house and all of the unpleasant memories that both held for her. But, while she felt relief at having to leave all of this behind her, she also felt a dreadful fear within her heart and mind. How would she manage alone? Where would she go?

It had been so long since she had been allowed to leave the house that the thought of doing so now terrified her. But she knew that it had got to be done, so the sooner she could gather her few belongings together and make a start on the next stage of her life, the better. She slowly sorted her few meagre belongings and put them into a large bag that would hold every thing that she owned in this world. She looked at how little she owned with sadness and relief in a funny way because she knew she hadn't the strength to carry anything very heavy, or very far and she had no idea of how long she would be travelling or, of how far she had to go.

There was one item of value however that she hid among her clothes and that was a silver photograph frame with a picture of her parents inside. This was the only item of value that she had been able to hide from her brother. It was her only link to her parents and to the happy memories of years gone by which she had never dared dwell on because it would have made her present misery seem even worse than it was.

It was a bright spring morning that she closed the once magnificent doors behind her for the last time and slowly started her journey into what she hoped would be a brighter future. She slowly walked through the avenue of oak trees that lined the long drive. Those trees had once been part of their play ground, they had often laughed and played hide and seek around them as children. But today it felt as if even the trees were bowing with sorrow and shedding tears. She took one final look back at the house, said, "Good-bye," and walked towards the road. This truly is where her journey would begin.

The birds were singing and the blossoms on the hedgerows were beginning to bloom. It was as if the world was welcoming her into a brighter future. She didn't look back again; she didn't want to see her brother's face at the window as he watched her leave. She felt no sorrow at leaving him after all, this, was all, his fault. It was up to him to make what he could of himself. She could do nothing more to help him.

As she neared the end of the drive she heard a man's voice calling to her. She thought it was Marcus, but no, it couldn't be. The voice was getting louder, it was becoming clearer.

"Annie, Annie, can you hear me?" "I do believe she is coming back to us," she heard the voice saying.

She slowly opened her eyes and tried to shield them from the light. She thought it was bright sunlight but no, it was light from a small hand held torch that the Doctor was using to see into her eyes with.

"Good, you are with us again," the Doctor said with relief. "You had us very worried for a while," he said.

"I thought you were my brother calling me to go back home," she said to him

"Is that where you have been Annie?" he asked

"Yes," she said and then she told a little of what she had been reliving in her dreams.

"If you ever feel the need to talk to anyone I am a very good listener," he told her. But in truth, he had a compelling urge to know more about her, he didn't understand why but he sensed the terrible mental pain that was exuding from her.

She thanked him and said that having some one to talk to might help her to come to terms with how her life had been up to this point.

When he and the nurse were in the corridor and out of Annie's hearing he confided that he knew he shouldn't become personally involved, but he felt sorry for her. From what little Annie had told him he had found it very difficult to believe that life could be so cruel to anyone, let alone a dear old lady like her.

He asked the nurse to organise a light meal for her because they needed now to build her strength up and get her back onto the road to recovery. He also decided to speak to a Social Services worker, who happened to be a friend of his. He wanted to get her into the system, so that when she was ready for discharge from the hospital she would have her own home to go to. He knew that it would be a few weeks before they could consider her discharge but he needed to get the ball rolling for her and the sooner the better.

A few days later Dr Howard sat and listened as she recounted old memories. He listened eagerly as she told him how life had been in her early days as a child and young woman. She described the people she had known, her home and many glamorous balls that they had held there. The garden parties in the summer and of course she had to tell him of her favourite pony. Her eyes seemed to fill with laughter as she spoke of the happy memories. But the sparkle left her eyes as she told him of the circumstances surrounding her parent's deaths. She also told him of the subsequent events which led to her losing both her brother and her home.

"Was there no one that could have helped you?' he asked as he felt compassion welling up inside himself for her. "Surely there had to be some one that you could turn to.

"No, there was no one," she replied. "Any friends that we may have had, Marcus turned against us when he became so rude and abusive to them all." "The only friends he wanted were the ones that he could drink and gamble with."

"I think that that is enough for today," he said. "You are still weak and I don't want to over tax you now." "I'll come and see you again as soon as I can when I'm off duty and you can tell me a little more of your story if you wish." With that he gently took her hand and said, "Good night."

For Annie it felt good to have some one that she could confide in. What a caring young man she thought to herself. Very different from the company she had been forced to live with on the streets. She was now feeling a lot stronger and somehow, she felt that maybe, at last, her life really was going to improve. For the first time in many years she felt she had friends, because here she had found people who truly cared what happened to her. Every one was so kind.

The nurse brought her a chicken sandwich and a cup of tea. "Try to eat all of this Annie," she said as she placed them on the tray now lying across her bed. It was a struggle but she managed to eat three quarters of the sandwich and drank all, of the cup of tea. Then she sank back into her pillows and for the first time since her admittance able to take notice of her surroundings. It was a cosy little room with biscuit coloured walls, floral curtains to the window and a matching floral screen that had been pushed back to the head of the bed. For her this comfort was a luxury that she had long forgotten.

Later, when the nurse came back to collect her plate and cup she told her that she was going to be moved into the main ward now that she was out of danger. There she would have people to talk to. In due course the porter arrived and wheeled her through into the main ward. Once in bed she settled down comfortably into her pillows and slept quite peacefully for the first time since her arrival.

She was awakened some time later by the sound of rattling cups and clattering trolleys. It was tea time.

"Hello Annie, I'm Wendy and I shall be looking after you now that you are here in the main ward," said a voice at the side of her bed.

Annie turned to see the smiling face of a young nurse standing beside her. She was a chubby girl with an infectious laugh. Annie took a liking to her immediately. "Would you like anything to eat?" she asked

"Yes please, I am beginning to feel quite hungry," said Annie "What have you got on the menu for me?"

"There is a nice piece of steamed cod, creamed potatoes, peas and parsley sauce here for you," she replied. "You still need to stay on a light diet while your stomach gets used to having good solid food inside you." "It must be a relief though, to have all of those horrible tubes removed"

Annie smiled, "Yes it's lovely," said Annie as she rubbed her arm where the I. V 's had been inserted. Wendy got Annie's meal from the trolley, gave it to her and carried on to the next patient. Oh! How much she enjoyed that meal. It was the first proper meal that she had eaten for longer than she cared to remember. She would certainly have had no complaints, no matter what they had put in front of her.

The next few hours slipped by un-noticed to her as she closed her eyes and slipped into a peaceful sleep. She was awakened later by the sound of footsteps going past her bed and the sound of people talking all around her. The ward seemed to have come to life as families and friends came in to visit the other patients. Every one seemed to have some one except her, but that didn't matter too much, she was used to being alone and lonely. But, that wasn't the case in here. Here she was made to feel important by all of the attention she received from all of the staff. She just wished that she felt well enough to perhaps, enjoy the attention a little more.

At last, visiting time was over and every one had gone, she was able to introduce herself to the other ladies on the ward. They all seemed to be quite friendly except for the young girl in the next bed. No one knew anything about her other than she had been brought in with a drug overdose. They didn't even know her name yet. She had been found in a derelict building by a policeman, who was now sitting at the side of her bed. The poor girl, thought Annie to herself. What could have happened to make her want to waste her life in that terrible way? She could only wonder.

The next day Dr Howard arrived with Mrs Patterson, the Social Care Worker. She was not a bit how Annie would have imagined her. No smart suit and sensible shoes. Instead here was a young woman in a long flowing skirt a pretty blouse and lots of clattering jewellery. I suppose it takes all sorts thought Annie to herself, but I suppose looks don't matter too much if she is able to do her job properly. Dr Howard made the introductions and asked Annie if she minded him staying with them while they talked.

"Of course I don't mind," she told him "I was hoping that you would get to visit me soon." "I know how busy you are and I don't want to interfere with your work but you are here now and it's lovely to see you and I want you to know how much I appreciate the time that you have spent with me." "I can't thank you enough," she told him.

"Tell me, how do you, feel today?' he asked her.

"I feel a lot better now that I can feed myself and I have got those horrible tubes out of my arm," she said with a tiny twinkle in her eye.

"It's good to see you looking so much better, but you do realise that we will soon have to look at your options for leaving us?" he said with a tinge of sadness in his voice and on that note. "I am going to hand you over to Mrs Patterson and let us see what she can do for your future well being."

"Oh! Please, call me Jean," she said to them both. "We don't need to stand on formalities."

"Would you mind telling me where you were living before the accident?" she asked. "Dr Howard said that you were homeless and living on the streets."

"Yes that's right," Annie replied sadly as she told her a little of the circumstance that had eventually led to her being here.

Jean's eyes were quite moist with tears when she asked Annie what had happened to her when she had to leave her home. "Where did you go to?" she asked.

"It's still quite a long story," said Annie as she went on to explain what happened next.

Chapter 4

She told Jean how she had walked for miles on that first day in the spring of 1938. It had been a beautiful bright morning as she started that long trudge looking for work. The first night she had slept on the ground in what appeared to be a coppice. It was bitterly cold but she was that exhausted she fell asleep almost immediately. The next morning she had awoken to the sound of the birds singing and the early morning sunlight trying to peep through the trees. Had her circumstances been different she would have noticed the beauty in her surroundings but as it was she could only think of today and what it might bring. She was hungry and thirsty but she had to go on.

It was only now, that she realised, that she had not eaten for more than 24 hours. She gathered her bits and pieces together and slowly trundled onto the road. As she began her journey again she knew that each step was taking her into her unknown future.

It must have been mid afternoon when she saw the sign saying staff wanted at the end of a pretty rhododendron lined drive way. She could only guess at the time because she didn't own a watch but she promised her self that she would buy one with her first week's wage. She turned into the drive way and as she started to approach the house her heart began to race within her, it felt fit to burst and she had to force her feet to carry her forward.

As she looked at the front of the house she was confronted with a beautiful Elizabethan style Manor House with variegated ivy growing up the walls. In places it had reached the tiny paned bedroom windows. All around the front door grew a pale yellow climbing rose it looked glorious. As she stood and looked at the house it appeared to be smiling, how welcoming it looked. She only hoped as she walked around to the door at the back of the house, that the people inside were as welcoming to strangers because she needed to rest. She needed food and drink, because by this time she was beginning to feel very faint and she didn't think that she could go one step further.

She put her hand out for the bell pull and as she did so she felt her strength leave her and a blackness enveloped her and she knew no more as her poor tired body fell to the floor. As she came to it was to the sound of a kettle whistling away merrily on the open range and a kind voice saying. "Are you alright my dear?"

She opened her eyes to find herself in a very busy but homely kitchen. She found out later that it was the cook who was holding her hand and gently patting the back of it.

"What a state you are in my dear." "Where on earth have you come from?" "What are you doing here?" The questions seemed endless.

"May I please have a drink of water?" Annie asked.

"You'll have more than that my dear," said the warm, motherly figure standing in front of her

"Maisie, make a strong sweet cup of tea my girl and be quick about it," she said to a young girl that was hovering behind her. "And as for you my dear, how long might it be since you ate a good meal?" she asked Annie.

"I think it was the day before yesterday," said Annie as she sipped the hot tea and took a huge bite out of a chunk of home made fruit cake that she had been given.

"Thank you so much for your kindness," said Annie.

"It's been so long since any one showed any sort of kindness to me." "I really do appreciate it," she said among tears of relief and tiredness.

"In answer to your questions, I saw the sign at the end of the drive saying that you need a house maid." "If the situation is still vacant I would like to apply for it," she said. "I'm sure that it is," she said as she turned to Maisie. "Go and tell the mistress that there is some one here who is interested in the housemaid's position."

"Yes Mrs Lawton," said Maisie as she scurried of to find the lady of the house.

"Now, my dear, wash your hands and face and comb your hair and try to make yourself a little more presentable," Mrs Lawton said to Annie as she poured some hot water from the kettle into the kitchen sink.

"Have you got anything clean to wear?" she asked

"Yes I've got a dress in my bag but it's very creased."

"Never mind I'll soon run the iron over it for you," said Mrs Lawton as she picked the flat iron up off the hearth.

When Maisie came back into the kitchen Annie didn't look like the same woman, with her hands and face spotless and her combed and pinned back behind her ears. Maisie was impressed with the transformation.

"The mistress will see you in the library." She said to her.

"Show her the way then Maisie," said cook. "And good luck to you my dear."

Annie was very glad that Maisie was there to show her the way because with all of these corridors spread out in front of her like a maze, she would have definitely got lost had she been on her own. Maisie was a friendly girl who chatted all the time that they were walking.

"What is the mistress like?" Annie asked her as they neared the library.

"Oh! Don't worry yourself about her," said Maisie, "She is a really nice person and very kind to the staff here." After a moments thought she said "We all think that she is what you might call, a real lady."

There wasn't time to say any thing else because they had reached the grand double doors that led to the library.

Maisie knocked on the door and then left to go about her duties leaving Annie standing nervously waiting for the lady of the house to call her in.

She didn't have to wait long before she was instructed to enter. Annie slowly pushed the door and walked in. How beautiful the room was. The walls covered in bookshelves which were crammed full of wonderful volumes of books. The wonderful rose wood desk standing in front of her but best of all was the feel of the thick carpet beneath her feet. This truly felt like paradise.

"Please sit down," said the lady as she sat behind that beautiful desk.

"I am Mrs Walker Browne, and you are?"

"Annie madam," she replied quietly and then repeated her name in full Anne Louise Barnett, but she explained that every one called her Annie.

"I'm pleased to meet you Annie, however if every one call you Annie, so shall I."

She thought pensively for a moment. Barnett. That name sounded familiar, but how annoying, she couldn't think why at the moment. Not to worry, it would come to her later, these things always do, she thought to herself.

"Maisie tells me that you are interested in the house maid's position, is that correct?" she asked.

"Yes madam, that's quite right." She replied.

"Please call me, Mrs Browne," she told Annie "l don't expect servility from my servants, only perhaps, a little respect she said. Please tell me a little about yourself and why you think that you might like to take this position.

"Please forgive me Mrs Browne, if I don't go into full details at the moment, because I find my past to painful to tell any one about at the present." "But please believe me I am an honest, trustworthy person, who is in desperate need of this position." "I had 15 years of experience thrust upon me, where I had to do every thing involved in running a house which was equally as large as this one." "Although if I might be permitted to say it was no where near as warm and inviting as this one is." Annie sat there for a moment looking around the room and taking in the beauty of it. She was especially intrigued with the books which were all filed in alphabetical order it must have taken months for some one to have sorted them like that. Then her eye was caught by an enormous vase of freshly cut flowers in the open hearth, in fact there seemed to be fresh flowers all around the room. They were on the desk in front of her, on a small corner table and even a small vase on each of the two windowsills in the room.

"'I see that you have noticed my weakness Annie," said Mrs Browne. "1 do like to smell the perfume of fresh flowers around the house and I do love looking at all of their beautiful colours, they always cheer me up should I be feeling a bit low." How different from the cold uninviting home that Annie had left behind her.

Chapter 5

Mrs Browne looked her straight in the eyes and said. "I would like to know a lot more about ou Annie, but it is painfully obvious that you are in need of the work." "I have decided to give you a months' trial, if after that time I find that you are not suitable, I will have to let you go and of course you will then have to find employment else where."

"Is that agreeable to you?" "Oh, yes Mrs Browne." "I don't know how to thank you, but I can assure you, you won't regret your decision," she said. Mrs Browne then rang the bell that sat by her right hand on top of the desk.

"I'll ask Maisie to show you to your room, where I think that you had better get some sleep." "You can begin your duties in the morning, bright and early."

Maisie arrived shortly afterwards. "Please show Anne to the room next to yours Maisie," said Mrs Browne. "In the mean time would you ask Mrs Lawton to find a uniform for Annie as soon as she can please Maisie?"

"Yes Mrs Browne," said Maisie and led Anne out of the room, back along the long corridor. They were almost back to the kitchen when

Maisie turned right and went up a narrow staircase which led to the servant's quarters.

"These are our stairs," Maisie explained. "The only time we use the main staircase is when we need to do the cleaning in the main upstairs rooms." "Normally they are only used by the family and any house guests that may be staying."

"Thank you Maisie," said Annie as she stepped into the attic room and closed the door behind her

Her room was sparse but clean. There was a single bed with a pink candlewick bedspread across it, one set of drawers and a wardrobe. The floor had been newly covered with linoleum with a small rug at the side of the bed. She looked around the room for a moment or two and then walked over to the window which was hung with pretty pink flowered curtains. The window looked out over the back of the house. She could see the well laid out lawns with there rose edged borders. The lawns were divided by a path that had, for its whole length, rose covered arches set at intervals. At the far end of the path on the left hand side was the kitchen garden and to the right there was a huge flower garden where even this early in the season she could see a rainbow of colour. It looked beautiful.

As she gazed out of that window she felt at peace with herself and the world for the first time in years. Then she turned away from the window and put her few belongings away in the draws and the wardrobe. She carefully lifted her beloved photograph and placed it on the top of the chest of drawers. She lovingly ran her fingers across it and murmured quietly to herself. "Well Mamma, maybe now I can start to make a new life for myself, I do hope so." She lay on the top of the bed and was asleep almost as soon as her head hit the pillow.

Next morning she was awakened at the crack of dawn as Maisie knocked on her door and called her name. "Come on Annie its time to get up, I've got your uniform here for you."

"Come in Maisie," she called.

Maisie entered with Annie's uniform all neatly pressed. "I hope it fits you all right, it looks as if it should." The girl who had it before you was roughly your size." "Don't be long now because breakfast is ready you don't want it to go cold."

"When you have eaten I'll show you what your duties are."

"Thank you very much." she said to Maisie. "I am sure that I am going to like working here very much and I am so grateful to every one for their kindness to me. Half an hour later and Annie was walking up the main staircase with a duster and dustpan and brush in her hands ready to begin what turned out to be a very happy time in her life. The hours were long and the work was, at times, very hard but she knew that what she did was appreciated and that fact alone made her feel good about herself.

Annie grew to love that house and all of the people in it. She had been kept so busy learning her duties and remembering where everywhere was that she hardly noticed the first month go by. It was now four weeks to the day and she was again summoned into the library where Mrs Browne was waiting for her.

"Come in and sit down," Mrs Browne told her.

She did as asked and sat there nervously with her hands together resting on her knees.

"Mrs Lawton tells me that she is very pleased with your standard of work and I must admit that I have no complaints either, so if you would like to stay on here the position is yours for as long as you would like it.

Annie was quite overcome with relief as she thanked Mrs Browne and assured her that she was more than happy to continue working for her.

"Good, that's settled then you may begin your duties immediately, but before you go there is something that I would like to ask you about your family," she said

Annie was rather un-nerved by this but her employer put her mind at ease. "What I wanted to know Annie, is this, have you a brother called Marcus and was he in France in 1914?"

"Yes," she said a little cautiously. "Do you mind if I ask why you are asking?"

"It would appear, from the information I was given, that my son Edward was killed at the same time that your brother was injured." "It turned out that they both joined the same regiment at the same time and they served their time together." "Edward mentioned Marcus in his letters that he managed to send to us, his father and I were so pleased that he had a friend there with him, it gave us a little comfort to know he wasn't among total strangers."

Annie was struck dumb founded as she listened to the facts that were being given to her. Why? Oh why? She wondered hadn't her brother shared these terrible times with some one. He should have shared his fears and anger. Then, maybe, just maybe, things could have been different for them. She continued to listen as Mrs Browne told her how the only thing that saved her brother's life was the fact that her dead son's body had lain on top of Marcus for hours. Any one looking for survivors at that time had very little chance of finding them because there were so many bodies of dead young soldiers all huddled together in one small trench.

Her mind was in a whirl, so much information to take in and what an enormous coincidence that she had literally stumbled into the one household that could answer the questions which had haunted her for so many years.

"I do hope that what information I have been able to give to you will go some way to helping you come to terms with the man that Marcus changed into." She said.

"I know that it has been a lot for you to take in, but I hope it will help you to think a little kindly towards your brother now." "You may go back to your duties Annie, but I suggest that you go and see Mrs Lawton first, for a nice cup of hot, sweet tea." "You had better tell her that I have sent you."

Annie slipped quietly out of the room and her employer continued with the paper work that was on the desk in front of her.

Chapter 6

Jean and the Doctor had sat in silence quite in awe of the determination of this frail old lady sitting beside them but Jean said that they had better talk about how she could help Annie with her present situation. She asked her if she had any financial means of support to which Annie replied that she hadn't. "I think that that should be the first thing that I get in place for you," said Jean. "There is also a sheltered accommodation that I know of, which isn't too far from here, so I will make enquiries about that when I get to the office tomorrow." Jean said.

"Thank you so much," said Annie. I appreciate every thing that you are trying to do for me. It's very kind of you.

"It's my job to try and care for vulnerable people like you Annie and I'm very hopeful that we can find some where that you like and that you will feel comfortable living in."

I must however point out that it will take a few weeks to get things sorted properly so in the mean time you will remain in hospital."

"That's correct," said the doctor. But you are not well enough to be discharged yet any way.

Perhaps you had better get some rest now, you are looking tired and I think that you better get some sleep," said the Doctor.

Jean told her that she would be back in a couple of days to let her know how things were progressing. Annie said her good byes to both of them and settled down in her bed for a well deserved sleep.

But, before she closed her eyes she glanced over at Claire's bed next to her, the curtain screen was drawn around the bed and she could hear faint muffled noises. There's nothing that I can do yet she thought to herself so she closed her eyes and drifted into a wonderful peaceful sleep.

After what seemed like only 5 minutes she was awakened Wendy taking her pulse and checking her blood pressure. "That's looking a lot better," she said under her breath. "That's good," said Annie

"Oh you're awake," said Wendy. "I was trying not to waken you, but now you are awake would you like a cup of tea?"

"That would be lovely," she said. "I am feeling a bit thirsty."

Wendy went to fetch her, a cup and Annie slipped out of her bed and went to sit at the side of Claire's bed now that the screen was drawn back. Claire was sedated and Annie didn't think that she was aware that she was holding her hand and gently stroking her brow. She wondered what circumstances had been responsible for this wretched poor young woman ending up in this state. It must have something really dreadful she thought to herself. But as she sat there holding her hand she made a promise to her, when she was able she would do something to help her. She was determined to help her get her life back on track and make something of herself.

Wendy came back with her tea and suggested that Annie sat in the chair at the side of her own bed while she drank it and because it was nearly time for the evening meal. Annie sat in her chair and pondered on the days events. How she hoped that Jean would be able to get everything sorted out for A short while after had eaten her meal she got out of the chair and into the bed and she had the best nights sleep that she'd had for a long, long time.

Next morning she sat at the side of Claire's bed as she had begun to do for the past 2 days. She would hold her hand and talk to her. She didn't know whether Claire was aware of her presence or not but she didn't mind because she didn't feel that that was important anyway. She just had this gut feeling that being there was important but she didn't know why. Wendy would come onto the ward and say "Are you there again Annie? I am pleased because I am sure that she is aware of you being there and I think that it will help her with her recovery" she said.

As she sat there Annie would describe the different visitors in full detail as they came and went in and out of the ward. She even had nick names for some of them. Mr Wilson would come to visit his wife in the corner bed and Annie called him Mr Bounce because he appeared to bounce along on his toes as he walked. She was fascinated sitting there watching him. Then there was Mr Davis his wife was in the bed opposite her. He'd bring in lots of fruit for his wife and sit there eating it himself while he was supposed to be talking to her. He was Mr Monkey because his favourite fruit seemed to be bananas. She was having a silent little giggle to herself when she realised that there was a hint of a smile on Claire's face, her eyes were slightly open and she was looking straight at Annie.

"Oh! my goodness your awake, how wonderful." "I'll ring the bell for the nurse."

"What's the matter?" asked Wendy as she hurried into the ward.

"Absolutely nothing," replied Annie. "Claire opened her eyes and smiled at me, so I thought that you had better know as soon as possible."

"Thank you Annie, if you would like to go to your own bed I will get the Doctor to come and examine Claire." Then she closed the curtain around Claire's bed.

The Doctor arrived shortly afterwards to examine her.

"Excellent" he said. "How do you feel?"

"A bit groggy," she confessed.

"Can you tell me your full name young lady and can you remember where you live?" he asked.

She told him what he wanted to know and he was satisfied with the way that she was able to respond to his questions.

"That is very good," he said with a smile as he turned to Wendy. "I think that we can get this young lady propped up in bed for a short while now nurse." "I will come and see you tomorrow when I am on my rounds," he said as he turned away from the bed to leave. Wendy did as instructed making very sure that Claire was comfortable before she left, but as she was passing Annie's bed she whispered to her. "I told you that it would help her didn't I?" And she had that lovely bright smile all over her face as she spoke.

Annie was content for now, perhaps her small effort had been rewarded after all.

The following day she heard the now familiar sound of jangling jewellery coming towards her. That has got to be Jean she thought to herself, I wonder what news she has for me. A moment later, Jean stood in front of her. "Oh! My, goodness," she declared. "How much better you are looking, it's wonderful to see that twinkle in your eyes," she said with a broad grin on her face. She sat down on the side of the bed and said happily. "I think that I have some news that will put a big smile on your face as well." "I have been able to acquire the flat that I told you about, if you are interested, it's only a short bus ride from here and about 10 minutes ride in the opposite direction into the city centre."

"How exciting" said Annie. "I would love to go and see it but I have no decent outside clothes to wear," she said.

"Don't worry about that, I took the liberty of buying you a new set of clothes, you look to be about the same size as my mother so I got her to buy them for you, I do hope that they will be alright."

"I am sure that they will." "It was very thoughtful of you to get them for me wasn't sure of your shoe size so I got you some sandals, your toes will be able to stick out at the top if they are too small" she said with a laugh.

Annie was only too pleased to accept her kind gift and to her surprise every thing was nearly a perfect fit,

"Dr Howard has given his permission for you to go, so we will have a word with the ward sister and then we can be on our way." Jean told her. She sat Annie in a wheel chair which she had left in the corridor and pushed her towards the front doors of the hospital and towards the promise of a contentment in life that up to now she had only dreamed about.

Annie could hardly contain her excitement as she sat in the front passenger seat of Jean's smart little purple car which was now speeding along and carrying her to her final destination. HOME.

Chapter 7

When they arrived the two ladies sat and viewed the quite imposing building in front of them. It had once been a gentleman's residence but was now split into 6 self contained flats. That one there is yours if you want it Jean said as she pointed to the window on the right hand side of the building. "Oh! It looks lovely from out side I can't wait to have a look inside." Annie replied.

So the two women got out of the car and walked towards the front door. Inside there were passages that led to each of the flats but the one to Annie's flat was the first one to the right of the door. Her heart was pounding slightly as she took those first steps towards her own front door.

"Here you are Annie?" asked Jean as she handed her a set of keys and she stood to one side to allow Annie room to open what she hoped would be Annie's own front door.

Once inside Annie walked slowly from room to room. She couldn't believe how spacious they were. She had first walked into an impressive lounge come dining room with its large bay window which she had seen from the outside. At the far end of the room were two doors. The one on the left led into a bright and airy kitchen with sparkling new white units, a washing machine already fitted and a gas cooker installed. She lovingly ran her hands over the marble looking worktops hardly able to believe what was in front of her eyes. They walked back into the lounge and then went through the other door which led to a pretty bedroom and a little further on to the clean sparkling white bathroom,

"I just can't believe it," she said to Jean.

"How do you think that you would like living here?"

Jean asked her.

"It would be wonderful," she replied.

"Good." "You have another look around while I go and make a phone call to organise some furniture, curtains and anything else that I think that you might need," said Jean.

She came back with a smile on her face. "That's organised," she said "Every thing will be done the day before you move in, so now we just need to get the date of your discharge from Dr Howard and then I can get the wheels in motion."

"You look very tired now, I think that this has been a little too much for you in one day and I think that I had better get you back so that you can get some rest."

Annie was only too pleased to do as Jean suggested and followed her slowly to the car. "I may be tired" said Annie. "But I am over whelmed with your kindness and the beautiful home that you have found for me." "I know that I shall be very happy there." She closed her eyes during the short journey back to the hospital and in her minds eye she saw a resemblance with the bedroom that she had just seen and the one she had when working in her friend Katherine Browne's household, for over the years a strong friendship did blossom and grow.

Nurse Wendy was waiting for Annie when she got back to the ward. She immediately got her into bed, took her blood pressure and a couple of blood samples. She then made some notes on the chart, gave Annie one of her usual sunny smiles and told her to get some rest now and said that she would be back later to see her. What a wonderful day she thought as she snuggled down into the bed, but oh! Dear me. How tired she felt and she closed her eyes with her mind still on the flat and thinking how lucky she was and went to sleep.

It wasn't long before the dreams came back and she found herself in her old bedroom at the Manor house. She had been there roughly two years when the Second World War broke out. The General volunteered his services leaving his wife to run the household alone, but he insisted that he may not be a young man any more but it was his duty to serve his country. Most of the young men who worked there had already enlisted and even young Maisie went to do her bit as she put it.

Mrs Browne made the decision to close most of the rooms in the house for the duration of the war. There was after all only, herself, Annie and Mrs Lawton still there so there was no point in keeping every thing as it had been, the house was just too big to do every thing that needed doing to it. During the long lonely evenings Mrs Browne often asked Annie to join her in the library and they would spend many hours talking about what was happening overseas and listening to the radio to find out any information that they could. And it was during this time that a special friendship began to blossom between the two women and when they were alone Mrs Browne insisted that Annie call her by her first name which was Katherine. Annie didn't think that it would be right for her to do that but her employer insisted.

"'The time has long since gone for us to stand on formalities," she said. "1 don't know about you Annie but I could do with a friend to talk to sometimes, I miss having my husband here to talk to and you and I get on so well together It makes sense don't you think?"

"You are right." Annie agreed. "And I would appreciate having some one that I could call a friend." The ladies sealed their pact with the last drop of sherry that was in the decanter.

It was on one of these pleasant evenings that Katherine said that she had an idea for helping the war effort. They had many acres of good land and she thought that they could turn at least 10 acres over to arable farm land. She had a contact who could arrange for 5 land army girls to work the land for them but of course Annie would have to supervise the whole operation, There was she believed an old tractor in one of the out buildings which would be a help if some one could drive it. So during the next few weeks Annie went from being a house maid to being a tractor driver come farm labourer. It was a wonderful time with the freedom ofthe out doors, although the work was very hard with extremely long hours but the girls who arrived to work the land were excellent workers and they were a jolly bunch to work with. Between them they turned what was, sculptured parkland into fields of corn in the summer and potatoes sugar beats and cabbages in the winter. They even managed to get a few head ofcattle and two pigs and half a dozen hens from a neighbouring farmer who's son's had enlisted in the army. He and his wife were too old to carry on with the farm so they were glad to sell the beasts to Katherine.

Every one worked from dawn to dusk but at the end of the day they would all sit around the kitchen table tucking into a good heart meal that they had grown themselves and Mrs Lawton had cooked for them. She made sure however that they all took their muddy boots off before she would allow them into her spotless kitchen. She wasn't going to have muddy footmarks over her clean floor. But she enjoyed the happy banter that the girls came out with and she enjoyed looking after them while they were away from their homes.

The next four years went by slowly as they waited for the end of the war and for news of their own loved ones who were away fighting in foreign lands. Their courage and patience was rewarded when at last they heard the wonderful news that the war was finally over and they could soon return to their own homes and get on with their own lives once more. How they celebrated when that final day arrived although it was tinged with sadness because they had in some ways become like a family. Each striving towards the same end to have done there part in keeping the home fires burning and helping to feed the people left at home. Katherine's husband came home shortly afterwards and was amazed at what his wife, Annie and the girls had accomplished. He was so proud of them all but especially proud of his dear wife.

Life began to get back to some normality during the coming months but slowly his health deteriorated until finally he had a stroke and died leaving Katherine totally alone. She had no family living there in Berkshire. Her only relative now was her brother who lived in London. Poor Katherine she was totally isolated and alone now, thank goodness she had Annie there with her to lean on she was the one person in the world who knew exactly how she felt and she always had the right words to say which were guaranteed to bring her some comfort. It was during one of the evenings that they were sitting talking together that Katherine said that she had an idea for their future. Because of her age Mrs Lawton was retiring and going to live with her son and daughter in law so there would only be the two of them living in that huge rambling house and to be honest since she lost her husband she had lost all of her interest in the estate. She wanted to know how Annie felt about moving to London with her, but not as a servant, as her companion.

They had, over the years gone through too much together for it to be any other way Katherine told her. Annie agreed to go with her because she also had nothing to hold her there. In due course the house had been put up for sale and the two ladies had packed all that they wanted for their new life in the city. Life it seemed was yet again going to take a completely different turn for them both, but at least this time neither of them would be left alone. From this moment onwards they would have each other for company and companionship and they were both looking forward to their new life in the city with excitement although it was tinged with a little trepidation for the unknown. But they needn't have been concerned because once they were safely ensconced in their new home they couldn't have wished for more. Life was good for both of them and Katherine now had regular visits from her brother which made Annie very happy for her.

Annie was amazed at the noisy hustle and bustle of the capital, it was a far cry from the comparative quiet of the country life that had been left behind them in Berkshire, but she had to admit that she was beginning to enjoy the new found freedom that this life with its' social whirl afforded her, They had been fortunate enough to find a beautiful Edwardian house near to Harley Street and they soon found themselves to be the centre of attention and invitations seemed to be flooding in for them to attend one function or another. Annie found herself wishing that she was a lot younger than her near 60 years of age. Maybe then she could have enjoyed the attention a little more. Oh! well c'est la vie she thought to herself as her dreaming stopped and she went into a deeper more peaceful sleep.

Chapter 8

S he was awakened the next morning by the now usual sounds of the ward coming alive. Wendy was there waking people up with her usual cheery smile. "Good morning every one," she said as she drew all of the curtains back from the windows allowing the light to flood in from outside.

"Who would like a nice cup of tea?" asked the lady with the tea trolley.

"Yes please," said every one almost in unison. They were all ready for that welcome morning drink of tea. Even Claire said that she would like to have a cup which made Annie turn and look at her in surprise.

"You must be feeling a lot better today," she said to her with a smile.

"I feel much better, thank you," she replied.

"I got out of bed yesterday while you were out and I had a walk down to the day room." "I will be able to leave here in a few days," she said as she swung her legs out of bed and got ready to sit in the chair.

She then asked Annie if she would walk with her down to the day room later because she wanted to talk to Annie about something important. She also told her that when she was very ill she did know that Annie had sat with her and she knew that she had held her hand. She couldn't acknowledge it at the time but being aware of her presence had meant so much. She had almost felt Annie willing her back to life and she too had felt that special bond between them, which she couldn't explain either.

"Well that doesn't matter," said Annie. "The important thing is that you are well on the road to recovery and we will have our talk later this afternoon when there is more time."

Annie was curious to know what Claire was going to tell her but she was content to wait until later to find out.

Later that morning the doctor arrived to do his rounds and as he approached Annie he had quite a grin on his face.

"Looks as if you have good news for me from that smile on your face," she said.

He nodded agreement and told her that she would be discharged the next day, now that he was satisfied that she had some where reasonable to live and he knew that there would be some one handy to keep a watchful eye on her. He also told her that he didn't want to see her in his hospital again as a patient she had got to take good care of herself. She took his hand in hers and promised that she would do every thing in her power to look after herself.

She also told him that if ever he found himself in need of a friend or if he should want anything he knew where he could find her.

He thanked her for her offer and promised her that he would remember what she had said. He felt very touched that this dear old lady had thought that some day she might be able to help him. What a dear soul she was he thought. As he reached the open door way out of the ward he turned and said "I will see you tomorrow before you leave," and with that he was gone to carry on with his day's work.

It was later that afternoon when Claire and Annie made their way to the day room. Good. It was empty and Claire hoped that it would stay that way for some time because she had a lot that she wanted to tell Annie. Fortunately the room was empty and they were able to find a relatively comfortable chair each which they put side by side and sat down. It took Claire a few minutes before she began to speak. She sat in silence searching her brain for the best way to begin her story. Annie knew how she was feeling. She was looking at a familiar sight in this young girl's eyes. How many times? She wondered to herself had she wanted to tell some one of her plight but could not find the words to begin.

Annie took Claire's hand in hers squeezed it gently and said. "Take as long as you need my dear, I have all the time in the world to listen to what you want to tell me"

Claire gave her a shy smile and said how pleased she was that she had met some one like her she felt as though she could really trust her and she badly needed a friend right now. A few moments longer Claire said that her boy friend Richard was going to visit her that evening and that is what was worrying her. It wasn't that she didn't want to see him, she did the point was she was terrified how she would react to him actually being there with her.

"I think," said Annie that you had better begin by telling me what has got you so concerned about this young man of yours. "I take it that he is the one you want to talk to me about."

"Yes and no," she replied. "It was something that Richard did that brought all of the old fears and feelings back, but he has absolutely no idea about what he did to me." Then she began to open up a little bit and told Annie she and Richard had been in her mother's kitchen where she was going to prepare a meal for him. She was at the kitchen sink preparing vegetables when he had quietly crept up behind her. He kissed her neck very gently and as she turned to respond to him he quickly guided her back into the corner of the units where he tried to kiss her on the mouth. His hands slowly moved down her body towards her thighs and that is when the old familiar feelings of panic, began welling up inside her. She had tried to push him away with out giving away what she was feeling. She had a smile on her face but inside her whole body was screaming for her to escape. She felt totally trapped, there was no where to go she couldn't move from the spot where she was standing. He must have sensed that there was something wrong though because he slowly moved back and looked at her with a questioning stare.

"What's wrong?" he asked as she quickly fled out of the kitchen, up the stairs and away from the danger that she had felt herself in. Poor Richard she had left him standing there on his own not knowing what on earth he had done wrong. He got his coat and left the house and that was the last time that she had seen him to speak to. She had watched him from her bedroom window as he walked down the road and out of sight. She lay on her bed for a short while sobbing into her pillow and wishing that she had been able to handle the situation better. She told Annie that she really liked Richard but he had inadvertently done exactly the same thing to her that her father had done to her many times over the past years and some thing in her had snapped that day. She said that she had been so pleased that he had stepped back when he did because if she had had a knife or some thing heavy to hand she was so afraid that she would have badly hurt Richard or she might even have killed him because she could feel her self control slipping away from her as he held her there.

Annie squeezed her hand a little tighter and then asked her if she would like to start at the beginning because she knew how important it was for her young friend to get her problem sorted out. She felt that Claire had no chance of making a relationship work unless she got all of these hidden feelings and experiences out in the open and if she wanted to have a loving relationship with Richard she will eventually need to tell him the whole truth, but for now that was for the future she felt.

Claire spoke softly as she told Annie that as a young child she had been adopted by a couple who couldn't have children of their own. She said that her maternal mother hadn't wanted to have her adopted but she couldn't afford to keep the baby and herself and her family had refused to give her any help. In fact as she found out years later it was her mother's family who had instigated the adoption in the first place and her mother had to go along with the family's wishes and she was now some one else's daughter. She told Annie how her new mother didn't ever show her any real affection, she felt most of the time that she was just some one who had to be tolerated. She couldn't remember ever having a cuddle or a hug from her mother and she wondered why they had bothered to adopt a child in the first place. She told Annie that nothing much happened in her life until she reached the age of eleven. Her mother had got an evening job as an usherette at the local cinema leaving herself and her father at home together three or four evenings a week. That was fine until one night when she had gone to bed and couldn't get to sleep; she had felt a little thirsty so she went down stairs in just her night dress. Father was sitting on the settee in front of the fire when she went into the kitchen for a drink. When she came out of the kitchen he told her to come and sit by the side of him which she did without thinking twice about it. He moved closer to her and put his arm along the back of the settee and he told her that he and her mother loved her very much. His arm slipped down from the back of the settee and he placed it around her shoulders. They sat there a little while not saying anything to one another. In her innocence she snuggled into his chest enjoying the closeness that she felt with him. Her eyes began to feel heavy as she snuggled there, close to going to sleep when she realised that some thing was wrong. His free hand was moving over her quite well developed young breast. What did he think he was doing? She frantically tried to push him away from her but her strength was no match for that of a grown man. He lifted her from the settee and placed her like a rag doll onto the hearth rug. He held both of her wrists above her head in one of his huge hands, lifted her nightdress as he began to fondle her all over her body. She had tried to scream at him to get away from her but his mouth was on hers kissing her in a way that she should never have known at that age. She remembered she couldn't breath, she couldn't move as his weight was on top of her as she felt the contours of his body against hers. Every thing after that was a blur she couldn't remember the specifics of what happened next but her body hurt her for days after that night. She recalled how the following morning her father had told her that she couldn't tell anyone about what had happened, it was their little secret and also if anyone found out about it he would be in trouble. She didn't want that. Did she? He asked

Annie put her arms around Claire and tried to comfort her as her body rocked with emotion. Annie tried to whisper words of comfort to her as she held her there in her arms. Eventually Claire regained some composure and told Annie that after that night her father had regularly had his way with her but he had always made sure that she was some where she couldn't escape his advances. She told Annie how she had tried to avoid being on her own with him but he always seemed to find the opportunity when it suited him.

"You poor girl," said Annie as she gently stroked Claire's head.

"Oh Annie, I am so pleased to have a friend that I can talk to about every thing." "I tried so hard to bury the memories and the feelings of hate and fear that I get when ever I see him but for some reason when Richard was with me that last time everything just seemed to come to a head."

Do you understand now why things happened the way that they did?"

"Yes." Claire replied. "You see he didn't know it but it was like a re-creation of past situations and I just flipped, I couldn't handle it any more" "The worst part was seeing Richard walking away from me with that hurt look on his face, he had no idea of what had happened." "That was when I decided that I didn't want to go on with my life any more." "I didn't want to face the future without him but I was so afraid of myself and what I might be capable of that I decided I was going to end it all. I suppose," she said that it wouldn't have been too bad if I could have talked to my mother about things but she had become increasingly aggressive towards her over the years. She had beaten her on numerous occasions and become very verbally abusive towards her. She said that she had thought for a few years now that her mother was aware of what her father was doing and that was her way of coping with it. In fact she told Annie that life at home was pretty grim and she couldn't wait to get away from her so called parents. That, she told her was why she had tried to take her own life. She no longer had the courage to fight her situation and thought that she would be better off dead.

"Where did you get the tablets from?" Annie asked her.

"That was the easy part," she said, her mother always had the bathroom cabinet full of pills, so she just grabbed a handful and swallowed them. If it hadn't been for her friend next door, who had seen Richard leaving and had come round to see her she would have managed to kill herself. But now she is glad that she didn't she told Annie because maybe now she has a chance to change her life for the better. Well, that is if she can talk to Richard about every thing and if he helps her get the professional help that she now realises she needs.

Annie was so pleased to hear her talking so positively and suggested that she fetch a nice cup of tea for them both. The afternoon had been traumatic enough for both of them but thankfully she hoped that this is one young girl who will have a happy future to look forward to.

Chapter 9

"My Goodness, where have you two been all afternoon?" the ward sister asked as soon as she saw them. "The doctor was here looking for you Annie, he wanted to give you a last check up before you left us tomorrow, but as we couldn't find you he said that he would call in tomorrow morning before you left us."

"I am sorry," said Annie but Claire and I needed to talk some where quietly, in confidence."

"All right Annie, no harm done," said the sister. "Lets have you both sitting down in your chairs; it's about time for your evening meals." "We don't want you missing out on those do we?' she asked with a friendly smile.

After the evening meal every one got into their bed and waited for those all important visitors to arrive.

Annie glanced over at Claire and with concern in her voice asked if she was feeling all right.

"I'm fine," she replied. "A little nervous of seeing Richard again but I am over the moon that he has decided to come and visit me." "I hope that he will forgive me for the way that I treated him," she said with a sigh.

She had no need to be concerned because as the ward doors opened she could see Richard standing at the front of the queue with a huge bouquet of flowers in his arms. His eyes searched the ward looking for her and when he saw her his face lit up and he almost ran to her bedside. He took her into his arms and kissed her cheek dropping the flowers onto the bed as he did so.

"I am so happy to see you looking so well," he told her. "I am sorry that I haven't been in to see you before now but I didn't know what had happened to you." "No one told me, it was only when I saw your next door neighbour this morning that I found out about you," he told her hugging her a little tighter.

"Richard, it's wonderful to see you," she told him as she felt herself holding tightly to him. "I was so afraid that I had lost you for ever," she said with the hint of a tear welling up in her eyes.

"There is no danger of that," he said as he sat beside her. "I don't understand what happened that day," he said "But I hope that you will feel able to explain everything to me and maybe we can work through things together."

She couldn't begin to tell him how much she appreciated his concern and she promised that when she was out of hospital she would tell him everything that had caused her so much pain and anguish in the past but for now she just wanted to enjoy the pleasure of his company and she leaned over to him and took his hand in hers, closed her eyes for a moment and breathed a deep sigh of relief and happiness. When she opened her eyes she found him looking at her with tenderness in his eyes and her heart melted.

She suddenly knew deep within her soul that here was the man who would be the love of her life and that he would always be with her standing at her side no matter what life threw at them.

When visiting time was over he said that he would return the next day and that he might have some good news to tell her. He wasn't going to tell her now what he was planning, she would have to wait a little while longer.

"Did you hear that Annie?' she asked her friend. "I can't wait until tomorrow to find out what he has in mind." "Anyway, what did you think of him?' she asked as she turned to look at Annie.

"From what little I saw of him, I thought that he seemed like a very nice young man," she replied. "I think that he will be very good for you and I have a feeling that he will always be there to look after you." "I think that you two were meant for each other, I'm sure that you will find a life time of happiness together," she said with a happy and contented mind sure that her young friend had reached the turning point in her young life.

Annie then settled herself down in her bed and waited for sleep to come and carry her into a peaceful world of her own because she also had tomorrow to look forward to. It would be the beginning of a long awaited time in her life, where she would be in complete control of her own destiny. She could hardly contain the excitement that she was feeling right at this moment.

The early morning hustle and bustle in the ward woke her up as usual, she could hear Wendy's cheerful voice at the other end of the ward, but as she lay there thinking of what today's events would be she suddenly became rather nervous. What a big step it was going to be for her but at least this time she would have the support of others and for that she felt very grateful. Wendy was soon standing at the side of her encouraging her to get out of bed quickly.

"Today is the big day," she said as she bustled around the bed. "We are all going to miss you Annie but we are all very happy for you and we wish you all the luck and happiness in the world." "I don't usually do this," she said as she leaned down and gave Annie a peck on the cheek.

"I am going to miss all of you as well," Annie replied. "I am so grateful for all of your kindness and consideration towards me and I hope it will be alright if I call in to see you all sometimes."

"That would be lovely," said Wendy. "We will all look forward to that but first of all we need to get you organised and ready because Jean will be here to collect you as soon as Dr Howard has discharged you."

It was about 9'oclock that the doctor came to see Annie.

"Every thing looks fine," he said. "Are you looking forward to today?" He asked.

Annie told him that she was and how excited and at the same time how nervous she felt about this next step that she was taking. Annie then thanked him for all that he had done for her and told him not to forget what she had said to him a few days earlier, she would be there for him if he ever needed her.

"I won't forget," he assured her as he turned to leave the ward. At the doorway he turned and raised his hand to her and then he was gone.

Annie was sitting saying goodbye to Claire when Jean arrived. "I want you to keep in touch and this is my address if you ever find yourself needing a home," she assured Claire. "Don't ever be afraid to ask for my help," she said. "You can always rely on my friendship, but I do hope that you and Richard make a go of things and that he will support you and encourage you in what ever you decide to do." Claire promised that she would keep in touch with her and she thanked her for giving her the strength to be honest with Richard and to do whatever was necessary to make a good life for them both.

"It's time to go," said Jean as she guided Annie out by the arm. They walked slowly out of the hospital doors and towards Jean's car parked on the car park. Jean put Annie's small bag into the boot of her car then she helped Annie into her seat, then she got into the car and started the engine. "That's it Annie, time to go."

It was a slightly overcast morning but Annie didn't mind that, her heart was pounding she couldn't wait to put that key that she was holding in her hand into the lock on her own front door.

"I hope that you don't mind," said Jean but I took the liberty of doing some shopping for you." "I bought Tea, sugar, milk, bread, butter and cheese so you can at least have a cup of tea and a sandwich while you are getting yourself sorted out".

"You are kind and so very thoughtful," she said to Jean. "I don't quite know how I would have managed without your help."

Within minutes they were there, standing out side her front door. She had no way of explaining to any one what this moment meant to her. She lifted her hand up to the lock and placed the key into the key hole; she turned it and walked in through her own front door for the first time in nearly 40 years. Finally she had a place that she could call her own.

"Go and sit down," she told Jean as she wandered into the kitchen. "I am going to make us a cup of tea." "The flat looks absolutely wonderful" she told Jean as she walked around the living room touching and feeling every thing. "It all looks so new" she said in amazement. "I never hoped for any thing this nice."

"Wait until you see your bedroom," Jean told her. "I think that you really will be surprised at what we have done for you in there." "Lets have this cup of tea first and then you can go and have a wander around on your own to see if you like what we have done for you, I do hope that you do."

They sat in silence for a while each deep in their own thoughts but both extremely happy with this outcome. Jean was so pleased that she had been able to make a difference for this dear old soul who needed her and Annie because she had truly found people who cared for her as a human being, it hadn't mattered to them that she was penniless, she was in need and that was all that they saw. How wonderful to have people like that in the world and she now knew them as her friends.

"That was a lovely cuppa," said Jean. "Now go and have a look at your bedroom and tell me if you like it." she said with a twinkle in her eye.

Annie took the new pair of slippers out of the bag that Jeans mother had bought for her as a house warming present, They felt like heaven on her feet so warm and comfortable. "I won't want to take these off my feet," she joked with Jean.

She walked slowly down to her room wondering just what Jean and her friends had done in there. When she opened her eyes she couldn't quite believe what she was looking at. The curtains and bedding were practically identical to those that she had had in her room at the manor house. Three of the walls had been painted a very soft pink and the fourth wall was filled with a painted mural of the garden she loved so much at the manor, which she had described in great detail to Jean. She stood in the middle of the room gazing at what was in front of her. She then made her way to the bed, sat on the side of it and sobbed with such tears of joy. She would never be able to thank these people enough she just hadn't the words to say to describe the way that she felt.

"I am so pleased that you like it,," said Jean as she poked her head around the door. "I have got to run now," she told Annie or she would be late for her net appointment. Annie got up off the bed and walked with Jean to the front door. "Thank you again," she said. "I am feeling overwhelmed at the moment and I think that it will take a while for it all to finally sink in."

"It's endings like these that make my work really worth while," Jean said to her as she walked along the corridor and out through the front door.

Annie sank into a comfy upholstered rocking chair which had been placed at the side of the hearth. She looked around her again and thought this is my own home. This is finally where I belong.

Chapter 10

A nnie quickly slipped into a comfortable daily routine of housework and the occasional walk to the local corner shop what pleasure these every day chores gave to her. No one except her closest friends would be able to understand what joy this gave to her. She looked forward to the weekly visits that she had from Jean (who always did her main shopping for her). Wendy, who popped in for a quick cup of tea on her way to work and she usually had a lovely bunch of flowers in her hand for her. "I know where the vase is," she would say chirpily and then place them on a small coffee table that Annie had at the side of her chair.

"You are a good girl to me," she would say to Wendy as she put her nose by the flowers and sniffed at their beautiful fragrance. "I am thinking of having a window box made for that front window so that I can grow a few flowers myself," she said.

"What a good idea," said Wendy. "I'll ask my husband if he can make you one, he's pretty useful with his hands," she said, with the usual twinkle in her eye.

"Alright," said Annie. "I'll leave that with you then thank you very much.

She had been living in her flat for about six months and she hadn't seen anything of Claire, she had had a couple of short letters from her but she felt increasingly worried about the girl. What if things had gone wrong for her again? What if she had done something silly again? These questions kept going around in Annie's head, how she wished that Claire would get in touch so that she could put her mind at rest. Two more weeks went by without her hearing anything and she was beginning to think that Claire had forgotten about her. How sad and how that thought hurt her. She had truly thought that they had formed a lasting friendship but how wrong can you be she chided herself for being so foolish. She made herself a cup of tea and sat in what was now her favourite chair. She placed the cup on the table and closed her eyes for a moment. And it was only a moment because the next thing she knew there was a loud knock on the door and the sound of people laughing. What on earth was happening out there she wondered? Who was making all of that noise? Before she opened the door she remembered what Jean had told her and put the safety chain on. She opened the door as far as it would go and what a shock she had, she couldn't believe her eyes. It was Claire and Richard.

"Wait a minute," she said as she closed the door and removed the safety chain. She flung the door wide open and Claire rushed in and gave her the biggest hug that she had ever had in her life. "How wonderful to see you both," she said. "I thought that you had forgotten me."

"How could I forget my best friend in the whole world?" said Claire. "You did so much for me that I can never thank you enough,," said Claire as she took Richard's hand in hers and gave him a loving smile.

"Come in both of you and sit down while I make you a cup of tea, or would you prefer coffee?" she asked.

"Tea is fine," they said in unison.

When they were settled in their seats Annie looked at Claire. "I can't believe that you are the same girl,," she said.

"You look so well and happy and I think that you have put on a little weight."

The two of them laughed happily. "You are quite right Annie, life has never been better for either of us" laughed Claire.

"Tell me all about it," Annie said. "I can see that you are dying to tell me."

Claire told Annie that the day after Richard had visited her in hospital he had finalised the details on a house that he was buying and that evening when he went to see Claire he had asked her if she would move in with him instead of going back to her mother's house. She said that she realised that this was the time to explain to Richard all about her past so that she could give him the chance to change his mind before they became too deeply attached. He had sat and listened to her story, he was obviously shocked by what she told him but it had made him more determined that she would never have to live in her parent's home again. Between them they had sorted out the professional help that Claire needed and Richard had accompanied her to every session, which had been instrumental in bringing them even closer together.

Annie could see that for herself as she looked at them it was if they were encompassed in a bubble of love that no one would ever be able to penetrate. How happy she felt for them. "I told you that he was the right one for you the first time that I saw him didn't I?"

She said to her young friend.

"I know and you were quite right," her friend replied.

"Does any one fancy another cup of tea?"

"I'm sorry that we haven't got anything stronger to celebrate with," said Annie with a huge grin all across her face.

"I'll make it," said Claire. "You talk to Richard."

They sat and made small talk for a moment or two and then Richard told her that he was going to ask Claire to marry him.

Annie was overjoyed for them both but she did ask him whether he was absolutely sure or not that that was what he wanted. He was absolutely sure and he whispered in Annie ear. "We have some special news that we want to share with you."

Annie gave him a knowing look. "Is that why she is gaining weight?"

He laughed and said "Yes that's right, we are going to have a baby but I really want us to be man and wife before the baby arrives," he said seriously.

"Have you asked her yet?" she enquired

"No I haven't, I wanted you to know before I asked her," he said just a little nervously.

"'I am thrilled about it," she said "but can I ask you if you have chosen a ring yet?"

Annie excused herself for a moment and went to her bedroom. She opened the top drawer of her dresser and took out a small, old leather covered box. She opened it carefully and gazed at the ring that should have been on her finger for the past sixty years. She didn't know whether these young people would like it but she felt that she would like to offer it to them. It needed to go to a couple who were so obviously in love. It had been hidden away for far too long and she knew in her heart that her Jamie would have agreed with her.

She walked slowly towards him with her hand outstretched holding the box.

"What's this?" he asked her with a curious look on his face.

"Open it," she told him

He opened the box slowly and couldn't believe his eyes. There nestling in the velvet interior of the box was the most beautiful pear cut ruby ring that he had ever seen.

It took his breath away. "That is so beautiful," he said to Annie. "I wish that I could afford something like that for Claire."

"You don't need to afford it," she told him quietly, because she didn't want Claire to overhear them. "I would be very happy if you would accept the ring for Claire," she told him.

"It was bought for me with so much love by my fiancé and it needs to go to some one who will treasure it the way I have for these many years.

Richard didn't know what to say, he never thought in his wildest dreams that he could afford something like that for the girl he loved.

"Will you take it please?' she asked him.

With tears of joy and unbelief he accepted and he put his arms around her gave her a kiss on the cheek and placed the ring in his pocket for later.

Claire came back into the room with the tea tray and put it down. "What have you two been plotting?" She asked because she could sense the emotion in the air.

"We don't know what you are talking about," they told her. But when she wasn't looking he gave Annie a big smile and a wink. They finished their tea and Richard said that they had to go he was taking Claire out for a meal later and they needed to get ready. They both kissed Annie on the cheek and left but before they shut the front door Richard put his head around it and told her that he would be in touch very shortly. Probably tomorrow he told her.

She sat in her chair thinking how happy she was about today's events, it had really lifted her spirits seeing those two so happy together. She felt tired but contented; she closed her eyes and allowed her mind to wander because now there were no memories to haunt her, no unhappy past to cloud her mind. Instead there was a bright peaceful light for her to follow and in the midst of it she could see Jamie with his arms outstretched and open wide waiting to greet her.

Her life's journey had ended but now was the time to make the one journey that she had waited a life time for. The one that she would take with Jamie at her side and this one would carry them into eternity together

Chapter 11

Richard looked at the clock which stood on the cabinet at the side of the bed, it was only 7 o'clock, but he couldn't contain his excitement any longer. He wanted to get to Annie's flat as soon as possible to share his good news with her. Claire had accepted his proposal and she was absolutely delighted to have Annie's engagement ring. It was the knowledge that Annie had wanted her to have her ring which had meant more to her than she could express in mere words and Richard couldn't wait any longer to tell Annie. He leaned over and kissed Claire tenderly on her lips, being very careful not to awaken her. He silently got himself dressed and went down stairs, put on his coat, opened the front door and went out into the cold morning air. He carefully closed the door behind him and headed in the direction of Annie's flat. He knew that Annie wouldn't mind an early morning visitor because she was always up and about at the crack of dawn. She had said to them many times that, "Her body clock had never recovered from the numerous years that she had spent in service."

"She had never been one for lying in bed and she wasn't about to start now," she would joke with them.

He hardly felt the pavement beneath his feet as they carried him swiftly towards his destination. He couldn't wait to see the look on Annie's face when he told her that they both wanted her to be guest of honour on their big day. He ran up the path in front of the house, went through the front door and turned to go to Annie's front door. He stopped dead in his tracks, the smile slipped from his face as he was confronted by Wendy knocking on the door and calling Annie's name. He could see from her actions and the distress he heard in her voice that something was very wrong. She suddenly became aware of him standing some distance behind her. She turned and ran to him sobbing that she couldn't get any answer from Annie and she had no way of getting in to see what was wrong. Why she didn't answer the door?

"That's alright." Richard assured her.

"I have a key we'll be inside in no time."

Wendy stood to one side as Richard opened the door. Both had the immense feeling of trepidation, both sensing what they were about to find. Richard told Wendy to wait by the door while he went in first. He called out to Annie as he walked towards her chair by the fire place and the words seemed to stick in his throat as he saw Annie slumped there, hands at her sides and her head bowed forwards. He turned to Wendy and the look on his face was enough, he didn't have to say anything, she knew that Annie was no longer with them. She had taken her final journey out of this world which had been so cruel to her. Wendy walked slowly over to where Annie sat, took her hand and checked for any vital signs, although she already knew from looking at her that she had passed away. Wendy rang for the Doctor and ambulance and she and Richard waited for their arrival.

They sat in silence for a few minutes deep in their own thoughts and remembering what Annie had meant to both of them. It was Richard who finally broke the silence between them both.

"I can't explain what it was about her that had such an impact on our lives." he said

"I never thought that any one could touch our hearts the way that she did after such a short time of knowing her."

"She meant more to us that our own families," he told Wendy in a faltering voice.

"I don't know how I am going to tell Claire, she is going to be absolutely devastated."

Wendy put her arm around his shoulder and told him that she knew exactly how he felt because she too had never known any one, who had touched her life as deeply as Annie had. They both sat on the sofa and waited for the ambulance and Doctor. They didn't have to wait long for the Doctor to arrive followed by the ambulance men. He pronounced the death and Annie's frail body was lifted gently onto a stretcher and taken away. They thanked the Doctor for coming so quickly and for the help he had given to them.

"If I can be of any other assistance please, don't be afraid to ask," he said as he turned to leave them.

Richard closed the door behind him and sank into the sofa before his knees buckled underneath him.

"I am going to put the kettle on and we are going to have a cup of tea," Wendy told him as she walked into the kitchen.

"Annie always had the kettle on ready, for when I arrived," she told Richard with just a faint hint of a smile as she remembered all of the mornings she had called in at Annie's on her way to work.

"My mornings will never be the same again," she said to him.

"I am going to miss her so much."

With that she disappeared into the kitchen and made them both a hot cup of strong, sweet tea which they drank in silence. When they had finished Wendy washed the cups and put every thing away that she had used. She looked around the kitchen with an approving eye. Yes, that is just how Annie would like it, all neat and tidy.

They said their 'goodbyes' outside of the front door. Wendy apologised for having to race away, but she was late for work. Richard felt as though his feet had turned to lead as he slowly made his way back home to Claire. When he finally got there his emotions got the better of him. He could no longer contain his tears and he couldn't hide the heart ache which he felt. He saw Claire sitting on the sofa with a blanket over her knees and a cup of coffee beside her on the small occasional table. He sat down next to her, holding her hand in his. He tried to tell her what had happened but his distress and tears seemed to flood the room with sadness. Claire looked at him with dismay.

"What's the matter?"

"What has happened?" she asked with an uncontrollable fear welling up inside her.

"Is it Annie?" she asked as her eyes filled uncontrollably with tears. She sat against Richard as he nodded his head in agreement; he took a deep breath and told her what had happened. He explained to her, how, he and Wendy had found Annie dead in her favourite chair. Claire put her arms around him and they clung to each other, joined together in grief at their loss but at the same time glad that they had a strong bond of love that would keep them together no matter what adversity they had to face.

When they finally managed to gather their thoughts together Richard said that he would ring Jean and make sure that she had been informed of what had happened. He rang her office and asked to speak to her. As soon as she spoke to him he realised from the sound of her voice that she had already been informed. She told him that the Doctor had rung her as a matter of course as Annie was in her care and she had no immediate family that he could contact. She also said that she would call to see them both to discuss the arrangements that she would be making for the funeral, although she would have to wait for the Coroner's report before she could do anything. They were not to worry. She knew how much Annie had meant to them and she would consult with them over the arrangements. Richard thanked her very much for her consideration and said that they would wait for her to contact them.

The day of the funeral arrived and Claire and Richard were surprised at the number of people who attended. The little church was nearly full of people, whose lives Annie had touched upon.

"I do wish Annie was here to see how much people thought of her," Claire whispered to Richard as they slowly walked into the little church which seemed to be full with the perfume of fresh flowers. They sat together in silence at the front of the little church holding on to each others hands for comfort and support. The words being spoken didn't register with them because they were lost in the depths of their grief. Claire looked down at the ring on her finger and her tears slipped uncontrollably down her cheek and onto her hand. If only Annie had seen her wearing it she thought to herself. It would have given her such pleasure.

A moment later she and Richard looked at one another in disbelief, they had both felt a hand upon their shoulders and they heard Annie tell them that she was there with them. They looked around but saw nothing but in that moment they knew that they hadn't lost her, she would always be watching over them and their tears of sorrow turned to tears of joy in the knowledge that she would never be far away from them.

Chapter 12

T wo months later Claire and Richard stood in the same little church where previously they had felt so much pain but today their hearts were filled to bursting with love, as they made their marriage vows to each other and they knew for certain, deep within themselves, that their unseen guest had pride of place amongst them.

They were blissfully happy as they settled into married life and their happiness was complete when three months later their son Michael Paul was born. They thought that there was nothing in this world that could spoil the life that they both now enjoyed as a family. So it was with uncertainty that Claire sat with Richard one evening and told him of the peculiar sense of fear that she had been having lately. She also told him that she had been aware of Annie close to her. She said that it felt as if Annie was trying to warn her of some impending disaster. Richard smiled at her and held her close saying that he was sure that things couldn't be that bad, he was positive that whatever she was feeling would go away and she would wonder why she had got herself so worked up about nothing. But over time the feeling wouldn't go away and she was aware of Annie's presence more and more over the next couple of days, then the thing that she dreaded most, happened, she had gone into Michael Paul's room to waken him but she couldn't. She shook him and called his name but there was no response from her son. She sank down to the floor cradling the still small body of her son in her arms, unable to believe that her son had been taken away from her.

"Why?"

"Oh why has God done this to us?" She kept asking herself.

She didn't know how long she had been sitting there on the floor when she heard Richard's key in the door. He had come home for his lunch, but how could she tell him what had happened. Richard called out to her in his usual chirpy voice.

"Where are you darling?"

"I'm starving."

"Is lunch ready?"

When she didn't answer him he looked around down stairs and then ran upstairs. As he reached their son's room he stopped dead in his tracks, unable to comprehend the sight in front of him. There was his darling wife, sitting on the floor cradling the lifeless body of their precious son. He walked over to them, lifting Claire off the floor and guiding her down stairs into the lounge. He sat her down before phoning for a doctor to come. He tried talking to Claire but she made no sound she just sat there with a glazed look in her eyes. He tried to take Michael Paul from her but she held onto his tiny body even tighter than before. She looked at him with such pain in her face that it nearly broke his heart. He wondered how he would ever get the strength to be strong for both of them because he felt absolutely shattered within himself. How could life be so cruel as to take such a beautiful little boy away from parents who loved him so much? How on earth were they going to cope with the pain of it? At this moment in time he just didn't know. He had no answers.

The doctor arrived within fifteen minutes of receiving the call closely followed by an ambulance crew but there was nothing that any of them could do. They took Michael Paul away from Claire and the doctor gave Claire a sedative to calm her down and to help her get some sleep. He told Richard that the police would have to be informed and that they would need to take a statement from them both. There would also have to be an autopsy he informed Richard, to which he nodded his agreement. The doctor then asked Richard if he would be able to take care of Claire over the next few days. Richard said "Yes" and said that he would ring his place of work and tell them what had happened. He had got some holidays due so he would be alright for having some time off work. Claire needed him so he would stay with her any way.

The next couple of weeks seemed to be lost in a blur. The only thing that they knew for sure was that they had each other. The grief and emptiness that they both felt drew them even closer together, but even as they supported one another they also knew that there was an unseen friend giving them the strength that they needed to face each new day. Each day was bringing them closer to the day that they were dreading, the day of their son's funeral. When that day arrived they clung to each other oblivious of the happenings around them. It was as if they were robots performing to a pre-set programme. At last the traumatic day was at an end and they were finally able to relax a little, but best of all as far as Richard was concerned, Claire wanted to talk to him about every thing that had happened.

Richard breathed a sigh of relief as he put his arm around his wife, she buried her head into his shoulder and she spoke softly about Michael Paul. She spoke of her love for her beautiful bright eyed son and how even if she had known what was going to happen she would have welcomed the short time that they had together. She also told Richard how much his love for her had meant and how it had helped her to cope and come to terms with the events of the past few weeks. She asked him if he had also been aware of Annie's presence at the funeral and around the home and he said that he had. He said that he believed that Annie knew what was going to happen and that was why they had been so aware of her presence before Michael Paul's death. They sat in silence for a few moments, each deep within their own thoughts and each hoping that Annie had been with Michael Paul when he died because they couldn't bear the thought of him being alone. Annie had been with this precious child, and at the time of his passing she had gently lifted his spirit into her arms and carried him towards the light and on into the Spirit World. There she had handed him over to his great grandmother who was also awaiting his arrival. She was any ones typical idea of a grand mother with her full rounded figure.

Her kind smiling face glowing with pride as she gently held her great grand son. Annie was sure that this dear, kind soul would watch over Michael Paul and help his spirit to grow. She knew that he would become a fine young man, one that his mother would be proud of.

Now the time was right for Annie to say "Goodbye," to her dear friends, not forever but for the foreseeable future. She stood and watched unseen for a moment as they slept entwined in each others arms. They were strong in their love for each other and she knew that the future held something beautiful for them. They would have their ups and downs as anyone would but the bond of love that held them was strong enough to cope with anything that this world could throw at them. She leaned over and kissed them both on the forehead and wished them sweet dreams. She knew that when Michael Paul was old enough he would visit them in dream state. He would tell them in his own way that he loved them and that he would never be far away from them. Annie said "Goodbye," turned and walked away into the light and back to her own life in the Spirit World where she knew that Jamie would be waiting for her.

Chapter 13

They stood hand in hand over looking the lush green valley where their cottage nestled snugly between the trees in a beautiful wooded area. They gazed contentedly at the scene before them. The light cool breeze played lovingly through her now thick dark curly hair. It was even more beautiful than Jamie remembered. They gazed adoringly at one another just as they had so many years ago on the earth plane, before Jamie had been so cruelly taken from her. How wonderful to be young again, she no longer had to contend with the confines of the frail old body which she'd had upon the Earth plane. She had no painful joints or restriction of movement of any form. Now they were both young again and were full of anticipation for the life of eternity which lay before them.

They wandered slowly down the hill side toward their pretty little cottage which seemed to be smiling a welcome to them as they approached it. The warm sun's rays like brilliant shafts of light dancing through the trees and hitting the window panes making them look like twinkling eyes in the bright sunlight. The white walls seemed to shimmer and come to life as she placed her hands upon them. She almost felt as if she could sense the heart beat within, as it welcomed her home. She couldn't understand what she was feeling but she was too tired to question it, she just needed to get some rest. Tomorrow would be soon enough to get answers to her many questions.

They entered into the cottage and she found herself in a very pretty but very busy room with it chintz curtains and matching soft furnishings. Under the window sat a pink chaise long and in the centre of the room stood a small mahogany dining table and four chairs. In the centre of the table stood a crystal vase filled with the most fragrant flowers that she could have ever imagined. The colours of the roses, sweet peas and chrysanthemums were so vibrant she wanted to touch them to make sure that they were real. The fragrance was quite heady and seemed to fill the room, how delightful it all was she thought. She sat for a moment to gather her thoughts and to take in the beauty that surrounded her. She closed her eyes and felt the energy emanating from every piece of furniture in the room. Everything seemed to have an energy source of its own and she could feel her own energy levels rising as she sat there. It felt as though she was as one with her surroundings. She tried to explain to Jamie what she was feeling but he just smiled and nodded his head in agreement and told her that he would try to give her an explanation tomorrow. But first it was time for her to get some rest because he had some wonderful things to show her when she was ready. He took her hand and led her upstairs to the bedroom, where she was in for yet another surprise. The walls in this room were the colour of the palest lavender flowers, the curtains and furniture were cool ivory. The bedding was a mixture of both colours with an ivory background and the tiniest of flowers dotted all over the duvet and pillows. She lay on top of the bed and fell asleep immediately. The energies in this room were totally different. Where the living room was bright, vibrant and full of energy this one was quiet and very tranquil but still feeling very much alive. She awoke feeling wonderfully refreshed from her sleep although she had no idea how long she had been asleep because in the spirit world there is no time. Unlike the Earth plane where life is ruled by the clock here, time has no importance. There is no day and night only never ending daylight because this is a world of light, the Summer Land.

Jamie was waiting for her when she awoke, and he told her that today he was going to show her some of the wonders of her new home. They went outside of the cottage into the bright sunlight. How warm it felt on there ethereal bodies and how beautiful every thing looked. As they stood side by side Jamie told her that now they had no need to walk any where. All she had to do was to think of where she wanted to go and in the blink of an eye she could be there. He told her to try it for herself, then, he pointed to the small marble seat which was the centre point of the garden. It sat in the shade of a flowering cherry tree and surrounded by the wonderful flower garden which Jamie had lovingly designed for her. She could hear the sound of birds singing all around her and butterflies seemed to be landing on every flower. This is truly paradise she thought to herself. She looked at the seat, thought about being beside it and in an instant she was there with Jamie at her side.

They sat in silence enjoying the beauty of their surroundings when Jamie turned to her and told her that he had always walked beside her. He had shared her darkest hours and laughed with her in her happiest times. He had been standing with her as she had gazed up at the night sky on so many occasions but her sorrow had been too deep for him to penetrate. He had desperately wanted her to know that he was with her. That he too, was sharing her sorrow, but he was unable to reach her. He said that he had watched the tears as they had fallen down her beautiful face and he had prayed that one day she would be aware of his presence but it wasn't to be. He told her that he had seen all of the traumas that had affected her through her earthly life. He had tried so hard to comfort her on the day that she had lost the home that she had shared with Katherine. He knew that Annie had taken a bus and gone on a shopping trip to the capital. He had shared her excitement as she spent most of her savings on new winter clothes and a pair of warm boots. She had had a wonderful day shopping and had treated herself to a meal in a classy restaurant. When she had finished she had decided to go for a walk in Hyde Park before getting the bus home. It was getting dusk and the park seemed to be deserted and she was enjoying the peace and quiet when suddenly, she had heard some one running towards her. The next thing she knew was that she felt a sharp pain on the back of her head and she was falling towards the floor. She had no memory of anything after that but Jamie told her that she had been mugged and that her shopping and purse had been stolen, thank goodness the thief didn't take her bag because her precious photograph and ring were inside. He told her how she had wondered the streets for days after that with no memory of who she was or where she lived. She had slept on the park benches and begged for a few coppers from strangers to keep her from starving.

He also told her that he knew how distraught she was and how he had tried to protect her all through the time that she was homeless. He said that he had been trying to talk to her that day when she had been involved in the accident and he blamed himself for it. Annie told him that he didn't need to blame himself because it was due to hitting her head during that accident that she regained her memory. It also had the effect of changing her life because through it she finally had the home of her own which she had always wanted and that she had found people who cared for her and loved her. She told him that she was very thankful that the accident happened. Jamie placed his arm around her shoulders and she rested her head on his chest as they sat in silence, each deep within their own thoughts, while enjoying the closeness of each other.

Chapter 14

The past days, weeks and months had been the worst experience that Richard and Claire had ever known since the death of their precious little son, but slowly they were beginning to come to terms with their loss and life had to continue for them both. Claire was now able to go into the nursery but her heart ached every time she remembered the times that she had cradled Michael Paul in her arms. Lovingly she re-arranged the teddies and other cuddly toys that were lying in the cot. She took a deep breath looked around the room and then turned and walked out of the nursery closing the door behind her. This ritual had become part of her daily routine and it helped her to get through the day which lay in front of her.

The following four years passed slowly in a mist of pain and sorrow for both Richard and his wife. Each day seeming to roll into the next with no relief from their heartache and the endless questions they asked themselves.

'Was it their fault?'

'Could they have done something to prevent the events of that fateful day?'

Of course they knew that they couldn't have changed what happened but it still didn't stop the thoughts that went around and around in their heads with relentless regularity. Today however, they would put these thoughts on one side because Michael Paul would have been four years old and they were going to his graveside to wish him a 'Happy Birthday'.

Here at least they could feel a little closer to their son. They put on their coats against the cold northerly wind which was blowing outside. Claire picked up the bunch of two dozen white roses and a small blue ceramic bear which she intended placing on his grave.

They closed the front door behind them, walked up the garden path and onto the pavement alongside the road which would lead them to the cemetery. They made the short walk in silence, each deep in thought of their own memories of their much loved baby boy. As they approached the cemetery gates the sun began to shine. It lit up the pathway between the headstones as if smiling a welcome to them. The sunlight played amongst the graves almost like a child laughing and playing hide and seek with them. As they stood in front of their son's grave the sun shone on the headstone lighting up the face of a cherub engraved upon it. She placed the flowers in a stone vase and stood the bear in front of the headstone and they both wished him a 'Happy Birthday' and they told him how much they wished that he was still with them. As they stood there with their arms around each other they suddenly became aware of another presence standing behind them. They looked around but could see no one but they were both aware of a strong feeling of strength and support which seemed to envelop them both. They were in no doubt that their unseen guest was Annie and they silently thanked her for being there. Her presence meant more to them than any one could imagine. She was their strength and their rock even if it was from the other side of life. Before they could leave Claire took a duster out of her pocket and polished the headstone until it shone in the sunlight. They stood together saying their last "Goodbyes", when Annie, whispered in their ears that tonight, they would have the first of their special dreams. She then kissed them on the cheek and left as quickly as she had arrived. They said a final "Goodbye" to their son and turned to walk away. When they reached the pathway they both looked back towards the grave and gave a gasp of disbelief, because lying along the top of the grave was a single yellow rose with its vibrant yellow petals nestled against the teddy bear. It hadn't been there when they had turned to walk away but now it lay so proudly along the length of the tiny grave. Now they had no doubt in their minds at all that it had been Annie standing with them today.

Words couldn't describe what they felt at that instant. They felt overwhelmed with joy, shock and with love, not only for their son but also for Annie. She was the dearest friend that any one could ever wish for. Their feet felt lighter as they took the short walk home. They didn't even notice that the sun had gone and had been replaced by that bitter cold wind which blew all around them.

Wendy was coming to visit them that afternoon after her shift had finished at the hospital. They couldn't wait to tell her of their experience that morning. Claire looked at the clock on the wall. It was nearly half past two.

"I had better put the kettle on," she said to Richard.

"Wendy will be here in a moment."

As predicted it was half past two by the clock when they heard a knock on the front door. Wendy stood there with a huge smile on her face and a big bunch of flowers in her hand.

"I thought you might need cheering up today," she said to them both as she put the bunch of flowers in Claire's hand.

"But it looks as though I was mistaken."

"I can't believe what I am seeing."

"You look so happy," declared Wendy with a huge smile on her face.

They both gave Wendy a big hug and told her to sit down and make herself comfortable because they had some thing wonderful to tell her. When she was settled they began to tell her about the events of their morning. Wendy sat open mouthed hardly able to take in what they were telling her, especially when they told her of the appearance of the rose.

"That's incredible," she said.

"I wish that I had been there to see it."

They sat talking together for another hour when Wendy said that she would have to go now but she would call in to see them the following month. Since Annie's death Wendy had visited them on a monthly basis. In the beginning she had just wanted to keep her eye on them to make sure that they were coping alright, but things changed and they had all become the closest of friends and Wendy looked forward to her visits with them as much as they looked forward to seeing her.

A little later that afternoon Richard told Claire to sit beside him because he had some thing important that he wished to discuss with her. He told her that he had of late become very dissatisfied with his work and he felt that he needed a change of direction. He said that he felt that they had both gained so much from their friendship with Wendy and it had made him realise that he needed to give something of himself to others. He felt the need to help others and he wanted to do it through nursing. He wanted to apply to become a trainee male nurse. Claire told him that she had had her suspicions that he wasn't happy at work and that she thought it was a wonderful idea and she would support his decision in any way that she could. She told him she had been considering finding employment for herself. She had seen an advertisement at a local care home which she wanted to apply for and told him that if she got the job she would be able to help support them both financially while he was studying. They held each other tight and vowed that from today they were going to move forward with their lives and that they would make the best of what the future held for them.

That night they had a strange feeling of contentment and exhaustion as they got into bed and they fell into a deep sleep immediately. They hadn't been asleep for very long when they both experienced the vision of their young son climbing onto the bed. How handsome he looked, he had inherited his father's dark hair and brown eyes but he had the soft facial features of his mother. He hugged them both and told them that he loved the teddy bear and the flowers that they had left for him. He whispered to them that he loved them very much but he was quite happy with his great grandma. He lay between them with his cheeks snuggled up to theirs and then he was gone. In the morning when they awoke their arms lay across each other, and between them was a child sized space and a small indent in the pillows. It hadn't been just a beautiful dream. Their darling son had really been with them. He had hugged them. He had kissed them. They felt the most incredible surge of love flow through their bodies and they realised for the first time since his death that now they could get on with their lives. They could start living again. What an incredible feeling of inner strength they both had. Now they would follow their dreams and they would do all of the things which they had always wanted to. Now they could finally stop feeling guilty about living their lives to the full.

Chapter 15

Richard's application had been accepted and he had settled in quickly to the nursing profession. He proved himself a real asset with his caring nature and his need to help others. He welcomed the challenge of each new day. What a difference the past four years had made to both he and Claire. Sadness no longer had a place in their lives it had finally been replaced by a new found joy for life and their love for one another had grown even stronger. In the beginning it had been a struggle financially while he studied and trained on the hospital wards, but he had loved every minute of it and he knew in his heart of hearts that this was the best decision that he had made. He had worked on most of the wards in the hospital to gain experience, some times working alongside Wendy. They had a particularly good working relationship which was very advantageous for their patients, partly because they knew for sure that they would always have something to laugh about. Both Richard and Wendy had the special gift of making any one feel better just by their presence. They were both extremely professional but also had the added bonus of an unmistakable gift for healing.

While Richard enjoyed working on which ever ward he was assigned to he decided that he would like to specialise in paediatric nursing. This was he felt, where he could give more of himself in helping the sick children to get well again. It gave him the greatest pleasure to see those happy faces leaving the hospital to go home. Sometimes it gave him great heart ache wishing that he was going home to Claire and his own child but it was only in fleeting moments because he was needed by these children and their parents. He and Claire were still trying for another child but it seemed that fate was not going to allow them to be parents to their own child and they had both come to terms with their situation although they both still lived in hope that one day it would happen.

Claire had managed to acquire the position at the local care home which she had seen advertised. She too looked forward to each working day because what wonderful characters they had there. It was extremely hard work both physically and mentally caring for the residents there but what satisfaction she got from it too. They gave her life extra purpose and she hoped that in some way she was able to give something of herself to them. While she helped care for all of the residents, she was the main carer to three residents in particular. Her two favourites were Helena and William. Helena a short plump woman with an infectious laugh had been widowed for many years. She and her husband Wilfred had been inseparable all of their married life and she had photographs of him all around her room. He had been a brewery drayman during his working life and although he worked in the brewing industry, he never touched a drop of beer. She would laugh about the fact that he couldn't stand the smell of beer, he would much rather have, a nice cup of tea. They had never had any children although they would have loved to have had a family and Claire often told her that she thought that she would have been a great mother. Perhaps that was why she felt such an affinity with her. Helena didn't dwell on the past and she would busy herself with her knitting and would, on occasion, keep the other residents happy by playing the piano and singing the old songs to them. She was a joy to be around.

William would often join her at the piano and they would sing duets together. He also loved the old songs and he would encourage every one to join in the singing with them. He was quite a character himself. Like Helena he had also been widowed for a number of years and his wife had been the centre of his world, but unlike her he had a family of three gorgeous daughters that he was very proud of and he spoke lovingly about them all. Unfortunately he didn't see much of his family now because they all lived some distance away. They were all married and had families of their own and his collection of photographs grew larger with each new great grand child that was born.

He had worked hard all of his life on the London docks and had many a story to tell of the large cargo ships that had come into port there. He would tell stories about the war ships and troop carriers which he saw during the last war. He said that he had even waved a last goodbye to his own brother from where he stood on the dockside and Claire could see a shadow of sadness as he recalled those times. He also told many tales of the beautiful passenger liners that came into dock and about celebrities and toffs that he had seen embark onto some of the ships. He kept her enthralled with every new story. He was a very knowledgeable man and Claire learned a lot from him about all sorts of subjects but the best thing about him was the fact that no matter what he spoke about or no matter how serious the subject at the end of it he always had a joke to tell. There wasn't a day that went past without him making her and everyone else laugh. He had the special gift of being able to laugh at himself and his own infirmities. He was as different as chalk is to cheese to the other resident in her care. Claire found him a very difficult man to care for because of his obnoxious attitude to her and every one around him. His name was Marcus Barnett but no one was allowed to address him by his Christian name. He always insisted on formality from people, whom Claire thought, he considered his inferiors.

Mr Barnett was a man in his late eighties, physically disabled and totally reliant on others for his care. Claire was the only carer who could get any where near to him but even so he would glare at her with those cruel piercing brown eyes of his. There didn't seem to be an ounce of compassion about him. She often tried to get him to talk about himself, but it was all in vain he would sit in his chair and totally ignore her. She tried asking him about his family, his mother, his father, had he any brothers or sisters? But he dismissed her questions with a wave of his old gnarled hands. He wanted to be left in peace and quiet he couldn't be bothered with all of these silly questions. As he tried to turn away from her Claire was suddenly struck by something remarkable. She could have sworn that she saw a family resemblance to her dear friend Annie. She couldn't put her finger on what it was but she could suddenly see Annie's face in his. It couldn't possibly be, she thought to herself, how could this, disagreeable man be any relation to such a wonderful person as Annie? She dismissed the thought as swiftly as she had thought it. Surely it was too much of a coincidence to have any relation of Annie's actually living in the home where she worked. To the best of her knowledge she couldn't remember Annie talking to her about a brother. He caught her looking at him and demanded to know what she was staring at.

"I am sorry," she said to him.

"I was just thinking about a dear friend that I used to know, something in your face reminded me of her."

"If you will excuse me I must go and see my other residents," she told him as she left his room, leaving him to his own solitude. The following few weeks went by without incident for both Claire and Richard but she couldn't stop a niggling feeling about Annie every time she looked at Mr Barnett. She decided that she wasn't going to worry about that now because she had more important things to think about, like the holiday that she and Richard had planned for the following week. While they both loved their jobs and the people who they worked with, they were looking forward to having some quality time on their own and the New Forrest would be ideal for them. They planned to have a quiet holiday with plenty of fresh air and country walks, but most of all they were looking forward to having time to be together. Their lifestyle now afforded them precious little time for each other and they were both missing that special closeness in their relationship and that was a situation that they were both eager to address.

Chapter 16

T heir week away had been everything that they could have wished for. Good food, plenty of fresh air and long walks in the warm July sunshine. They sat on a grassy bank beneath a tall oak tree and Richard leaned towards her and whispered his never ending love in her ear. She responded by giving him a warm sensual kiss and they both rejoiced in the knowledge of their undying love for each other.

"How lucky we are to have each other," Richard said, as they stood up ready to make their way back to the holiday chalet and the unfinished packing which was waiting for them.

"What a wonderful time it has been," said Claire.

"But I am ready to go home now and it will be good to get back to work on Monday."

"It's great to get away for a while but it's even better to get back to our own little house and our usual daily routine.".

Monday morning found Claire and Richard kissing each other goodbye as they headed in different directions towards their places of work. They each felt lightness in their step and a renewed vitality within themselves. Their week away had done them both the world of good and they were ready to face their daily tasks with a renewed vitality and energy.

Claire walked into work at the care home with a huge smile on her face and there was nothing and no one that was going to upset her today. Not even grumpy old Mr Barnett was going have any effect on her she thought to herself as she approached the residents lounge. She walked through the door and immediately sensed that something was not as it should be. She looked over at William and Helena who were sitting in front of the bay window. William beckoned to her and as she approached him he whispered that she needed to go to Mr Barnett's room. She thanked him, turned and went quickly to Mr Barnett's room. There she found him lying in his bed with a nurse and a doctor in attendance. She knew from experience that he didn't have much longer to be here on the Earth plane. It was almost time for his journey upon the Earth to finish. The nurse asked her to stay with her patient while she and the doctor left the room to discuss the necessary steps to take next.

While they were gone Claire touched his hand and asked him if he knew it was her. He nodded and she thought that she saw a shadow of a smile pass over his face but it was gone again in an instant.

"Can I do anything to make you more comfortable?" She asked him

But he didn't seem to hear her. He was staring at some thing in the corner of the room; his eyes seemed to be transfixed and for the first time since she had known him, his hard cruel features seemed to soften for an instant. He lifted a bony hand and pointed to the corner. His lips and mouth moved as though he was trying to say something.

But the only sound that came from him was a hardly audible "A-A-A-A". Was he trying to say Annie? Claire wondered to herself could this obnoxious old man really be a relative of such a wonderful person as her dear friend Annie?

As he held his hand out towards the corner of the room Claire noticed that he had what looked like an old torn sepia coloured photograph clutched between his fingers. She had never seen the photograph before and was curious to know where he had been hiding it, but decided that that was the last thing that she needed to know. Claire followed the direction of his hand with her eyes and was amazed to become suddenly aware of a bright light shining in the corner. It was hovering towards the ceiling and Claire thought that she could hear her friend's voice telling her that this old man was indeed her brother and that she had come to watch over his passing into the Spirit World.

As she stood looking at the light Claire could see the face and form of her dear friend slowly begin to build in front of her. Her joy at seeing her friend was overwhelming but then her attention was drawn to the bed and the man lying there. She walked back towards him and suddenly, without warning his quiet composure was interrupted when he started throwing his arms wildly about. Claire couldn't understand the change in him and the absolute terror which had seemed to engulf him. He was trying to push something or someone away but it was to no avail. Suddenly there was a cold rush of air and a terrifying darkness filled the room. The blackness enveloped him and then he was gone. Claire looked towards the place where she had seen Annie only a moment before but now the space was empty and she felt utterly alone with the still lifeless body before her.

She called the nurse and the doctor back into the room. He examined the body for any signs of life before recording the time of death. He and the nurse then completed all of the formalities before he left to return to his surgery and the rest of his day's work. The nurse asked Claire to help her to lay the body out in preparation for the funeral directors to collect. She opened his hand to reveal a battered and torn old photograph showing a small girl of about eight years of age standing at the side of what she thought was a dappled grey pony. She was standing holding the reins in her right hand and her left hand was draped over the pony's neck. What a pretty child she was with her long black hair cascading down her back beneath her riding hat. Her pretty, frilly calf length dress showed off her side buttoning boots. It must have been a treasured memory Claire thought to herself as she placed the photograph back into his hand so that it could make the final journey with its owner.

When she got home Claire sank into the cream leather sofa and let out a huge sigh of relief.

"What a day it's been!" she said to Richard when he arrived home shortly after her.

"Why?"

"What's happened?" he asked her.

She relayed all of the events of the day to him and told him that she didn't want to go through another day like that for some time to come.

"Come here," he said.

As he held her close to him giving her the comfort that she so badly needed at that time.

"What would I do without you?" she murmured as he held her closer to him and kissed her tenderly on the mouth.

"You can get your coat for a start," he said with a twinkle in his eye.

"It's been a hard day and I am taking you out for dinner."

Claire was only too happy to oblige because she didn't fancy the thought of having to stand in the kitchen cooking their evening meal. What a traumatic day it had turned out to be and it had taken a lot more out of her than she had at first realised.

They decided that it would be a nice change to go to the local Italian restaurant which was their favourite. They sat at their usual corner table which was quite romantic with the dimmed lights and soft music playing in the background. Every table had a small cut glass vase in the centre which held a single white rose. All of the table cloths shone with a pristine white condition and across the top of each table ran a deep red runner. The whole ambiance was just what she needed and the meal was cooked to perfection.

She leaned across the table towards Richard and thanked him for his loving consideration.

Richard looked at his wife and told her that he had decided to take her out tonight anyway because he had some wonderful news to share with her. Claire suddenly felt excited for him. She knew that he had spent hours and hours studying for his next exam over the past few weeks. He filled their glasses from the bottle of their favourite wine which stood in the cooled bucket at the side of him. He asked her to join him as he raised his glass and told her that he had received the results today of the latest exam that he had been studying and that she was now married to the new senior staff nurse. Claire was so excited for him she could hardly contain herself. She wanted to throw her arms around her husband and give him the biggest kiss, but instead she contented herself by telling him how proud she was of him and of all that he had achieved. He told her how grateful he was to her for all of the support and encouragement she had given to him and that he could never have done it without her. They raised their glasses once more and said in unison.

"To us and our future."

Chapter 17

The following five years passed by almost un-noticed as both Richard and Claire became more and more involved with their working lives. They both found enormous satisfaction in what they did but in totally different ways. For Richard there was great joy every time he saw a child come onto his ward regain their health and instead of tears and pain, he saw wonderful smiles from happy, healthy children. Sometimes though, there was heart ache. Times when he didn't feel that he had done enough to help the children, but he realised that he had to resign himself to the fact that he was only human and that there was only so much that he could do within the boundaries of his job. It still pulled on the heart strings when he had to face the grief of heart broken families. He had a gentle way of dealing with distraught parents because of what he and Claire had gone through. He understood their pain and he had a wonderful way of helping them to deal with their traumatic experience.

Claire too had times of joy and sadness at the care home. William and Helena had continued to entertain the other residents with their music and singing sessions on a Thursday afternoon. Today was like any other Thursday as Claire began her afternoon shift. As she entered the sitting room she expected to hear every one having a sing song as usual, but today there was nothing. There was no sign of William and Helena was sitting alone by the window, staring into space. Claire approached her and asked gently what had happened. Helena looked up at her and Claire could see the tears rolling down her sad, lined face. She suddenly looked very old and the twinkle had gone out of her eyes.

Claire put her arms around Helena to comfort her before she asked her, why she was so upset?

She looked into Claire's eyes and whispered.

"He has gone."

"What do you mean?" asked Claire.

"Who has gone?"

"William has, he came down for breakfast this morning and keeled over at the table."

"He had a heart attack and died, it was dreadful," she said as she buried her head into her hands and sobbed quietly to herself, not wishing to talk anymore.

Claire rushed out of the room and headed towards the matron's office, she needed to know what had happened for her own peace of mind. She couldn't imagine not being greeted by his lovely smiling face when she walked into work. The world will be a poorer place for not having him in it she thought to herself. As Claire approached the office she could see the undertakers taking William's body out through the rear entrance and her heart sank a little.

"Things just won't be the same around here any more," she whispered to herself.

But she knew that this was something to be expected. It was all part of the work and she knew that she couldn't afford to take William's passing into the Spirit World too much to heart.

Matron was sitting at her desk sorting out the day's paperwork when Claire walked in.

She looked up at Claire and beckoned towards the chair which was placed in front of her desk. She told Claire to sit down and then proceeded to explain what had happened. She said that the family had been informed and that they were due to arrive the following day. She asked Claire to pack all of William's belongings so that they would be ready for the family to collect. Claire went to his room and carefully packed personal belongings into a suitcase which he kept in the wardrobe. She placed his precious photographs together with other sundry items on the top of the freshly made bed. She made an inventory of all of his belongings which she gave to the Matron who would give it to the family the next day. While Claire waited for the cleaning staff to finish in William's room she went into the garden and picked a bunch of lavender which she knew was William's favourite flower. He said that the perfume reminded him of his dear wife. Claire put the lavender into a crystal glass vase and placed it on the bedside cabinet and then walked towards the door. She took one last look and with great sadness closed the door behind her. Now she had to think of the other residents and take care of their needs, they were the important ones now.

That night as she climbed the stairs, Claire wished that Richard was at home with her, but he was on night shift at the hospital and he wouldn't get home until the morning. She softly sighed to herself and accepted the inevitability of a night alone. She fell into restless sleep thinking about the day's events and the sadness which had engulfed the care home. She eventually sank into a more restful sleep and started to dream of happier times. She could see William sitting on the bench in the flower garden at the home and beside him sat Michael Paul. As she walked swiftly towards them William rose from his seat. He smiled and waved goodbye and disappeared in front of her. She sat on the bench beside her son, taking his hand in hers. She reflected on how blessed she was to have these dreams and to know with certainty that he would never be far away from either her or his father.

As they sat together Michael Paul turned to his mother with a look of sadness on his face and kept repeating the words.

"I'm sorry mummy."

"What do you mean Michael?"

"Why should you be sorry?" She asked him.

But he said no more, he leaned against her, told her how much he loved her and was gone.

When she awoke the next morning she was totally bewildered by what her son had said to her. What on earth would make him sorry about anything she wondered? When Richard came home she gave him his breakfast and over a cup of tea she told him of her dream. He was as bewildered as her but told her not to worry too much about it she was probably getting things mixed up in her mind he assured her. A short time later Claire put on her over coat kissed her husband goodbye and walked towards the front door ready to begin another day at work. She was putting her hand out to reach the door handle when she shouted out in pain. Richard found her crumpled up on the floor clutching her stomach. He immediately rang for a taxi and got her to the hospital as quickly as possible. Claire was rushed to theatre where it was discovered that she was having an ectopic pregnancy and she was in danger of the fallopian tube bursting. After an emergency operation she was safely placed in the recovery room and Richard was then informed of what had happened to his wife. He was devastated. How could he possibly tell his darling wife what had happened to her? But he knew that she had to be told and that he was the one to tell her.

He sat at her bedside holding her hand and waiting for her to recover enough for him to talk to her. When she finally awoke and asked him what had happened. He held her in his arms and explained to her that she had lost a baby, which neither of them had realised that she was carrying. They held on tightly to each other, their tears of sorrow mingling together. He told her that the most important thing to him was that she was going to be alright and that he would make sure that she would never have to go through that again. At that moment they resigned themselves to the fact that they would never be parents, no matter how much they wanted to be. Richard was not going to risk the health of this wonderful woman that he was married to. A few days later Claire was released from hospital into Richard's care. That evening as they sat at home in front of a warm cosy fire, they sat and talked of their loss and of the possibility of never having a family of their own. They realised how dangerous it could possibly be to Claire's health and they both agreed that they couldn't face the thought of losing another child. They decided that they would face the world together and not look back to what might have been. It was the hardest decision that they had had to make in their life together, but never the less they felt that at this time it was the right choice to make. Richard fetched a bottle of their favourite wine from the kitchen and poured a glass for them both. He looked lovingly at his wife lifted his glass and said.

"Let's make a toast."

"To the future and to us."

Claire raised her glass with her husband with a sadness hidden deep within her which she hoped that time would heal.

"To the future and to us," she repeated as she leaned towards her husband and clung to him in a passionate embrace.

Chapter 18

After her brother's death Annie returned to the spirit world with an overpowering feeling of sadness. If only she could have been the one to take her brother back to the world of light instead of those dark frightening entities from the lower realms being the ones to collect his immortal spirit. No matter what he had done to her or how he had hurt her during her life upon the earth it couldn't stop her love for him. She couldn't forget the look of terror on his face as he saw them. She had been swept to one side by their ugliness, their cold disrespect for the soul that had once been her brother. Her very being cried out for him but it was to no avail. It was as if they hadn't even been aware of her presence in the room.

"If only there was some thing that I could do to help him" she said to Jamie as he held her and tried to console her in any way that he could think of but his words landed on deaf ears. So then he reminded her of the facts that she already knew, that their life had to continue and that she had a lot of work still to do. There were so many souls on the earth who needed her to be there at their passing. They needed her to give them peace of mind and to reassure them of their life yet to come. She had to show them the way back to their spiritual home. He also reminded her of how important his presence was at her passing and that she was needed for all those other souls, for whom, their time was yet to come.

Annie had visited Claire and Richard many times during the last five years but neither of them had been aware of her presence around them and while this fact brought her sorrow it also brought her great joy to see her friends happy and contented in their earthly lives.

Life in the spirit world settled into a routine for both Annie and Jamie. Each doing the work which they loved, but no matter how much satisfaction Annie found in her work, she couldn't erase the memory of her brother's passing from the Earth Plane to the Spirit World. Annie knew deep within her soul that the sisterly love which she felt for Marcus wouldn't allow her to leave him languishing in the darkness of his own despair. She remembered with fondness the brother she knew as a child, not the stranger who had returned to the family after the war. She had forgiven him long ago for the cruelty he had shown towards her during those horrible years that they were together. She had come to realise that he had no control over his actions and she wished that she had tried to do more to help him at the time but she didn't know what it was that she could have done. Life had been very cruel to both of them but perhaps now she could do something positive to help him overcome his present situation.

Annie knew that she would need a special dispensation from the Committee of Elders to enter the lower regions of spirit, which is where she would need to go if she had any chance of helping him. As she could not approach the Committee directly she would ask

Nathaniel, the Guardian of the Book of Souls to arrange an audience with the Committee on her behalf. Nathaniel agreed to try and arrange it for her but he warned her that it would be most unusual for the Committee to agree to such a request, but he could see how much it meant to her and he would try his best to persuade the Committee to allow her to state her case before them. He had argued her case passionately before them and had secured an appointment for her the next day.

As Annie knocked upon the huge double doors to the entrance hall of the committee chamber she was filled with trepidation which eased slightly when Nathaniel opened the door to her. He showed her into the chamber and took her to the centre of the room where she stood in a circular area surrounded by tiers of seats which rose high into the air. Today however, only five seats were occupied and they were situated immediately in front of where she stood. She raised her eyes to see the occupants of these seats but the brightness surrounding them blinded her for a second and she needed to shield her eyes from the light which emanated from them. While her eyes became accustomed to the light Nathaniel guided her to a chair and told her to sit down. The Elders gave her a few moments for her eyes to become adjusted to the light, and then the senior Elder asked her why she had asked for this audience with them.

Annie explained to them why she was there and the reasons why she wanted their permission to enter the lower regions to try and help her brother. She explained to them that she didn't feel that Marcus should be left in the lower regions with out any one to help him.

"He is a kind and loving person by nature," she told them.

"It was the effects that the war had on him during his life on earth that made him the cruel, callous person which she admitted that he had become."

She explained that he desperately needed help and she wanted to volunteer to go to the lower region to help him. She told them that she couldn't help him while on the Earth Plane but perhaps now that the confines of the material body were gone she could find a way to help him.

The Elders listened to her arguments for going to Marcus's aid intensely and then asked her to leave the room while they conferred among themselves. They told her to wait outside and they would call her in when they were ready. She rose from the chair and thanked them for their consideration and then left the room. Nathaniel sat with her to give her the courage which he knew that she would need should the Elders agree to her request. She didn't have to wait for long before she was summoned before them again. She stood nervously before them as she awaited their answer. The leader of the Elders who had been sitting in the centre of the five spoke gently to her.

"We have all agreed to allow you to try to help your brother as we can see how important he is to you but we must warn you that when you commence your journey to the lower levels you will be on your own."

"There will be no help for you from this level."

"We tell you this, because we want you to realise exactly what dangers you will be facing."

"You will be in danger of being drawn into the darkness yourself."

"The depressing atmosphere you will encounter will be extremely powerful and you may not have the strength to combat it alone."

"The only way that you will be able to return to this level, where you belong, is if you can get through to your brother and he, himself asks for the help that you will both need."

"I don't want to frighten you," he said.

"But I do want you to be aware of the dangers which you will face."

Annie looked into his kindly eyes and thanked him for his concern but she assured him that she was prepared to do what ever it took to help her brother. She said that she fully understood the danger in which she was placing herself and she was prepared to accept the consequences of her actions if she couldn't accomplish what she had set out to do. She also told them that she had discussed her intensions with Jamie and that he had reluctantly given her his blessing to embark on this terrible quest.

A few days later Annie and Jamie sat on the hillside overlooking their beautiful home and the lush green surrounding it. Annie wanted to keep this wonderful view fresh in her memory as a reminder of what she had left behind when she was in the dark oppressive lower levels of the Spirit World. Finally she turned to Jamie and told him that she was ready to begin her journey. He held her close to him, kissed her lovingly and said that he would pray for her safe return to him. He smiled at her but she could see the beginnings of tears in his eyes as she walked away from him. She knew that his smile would be the last beautiful thing that she would see.

Her journey to the lower levels was the most frightening experience that she had ever had. She could feel the cold heaviness of oppression getting stronger around her as she descended to where Marcus existed. The only light that she could see as she entered this level was the light that shone from her own spirituality. Darkness seemed to engulf her as she stood at the entrance to the drive way which led to the house that she knew so well. She stood and gazed at the familiar sight of the huge oak tree lined drive but now the trees stood like skeletal silhouettes against the darkness which surrounded them. No longer could she hear bird song from their branches as she did in her childhood. All she could see now was a dark depressing ugliness all around her. She trod carefully along the drive way trying to avoid the broken branches which appeared to lie along its length. She felt an unnerving eeriness as she walked towards the house. Her nerves began to tingle as she felt unseen eyes watching her. Finally she reached what used to be a beautiful, heavy oak door at the front of the house but what she was confronted with made her heart sink. It hung half off its' hinges, and the once shiny brass knocker was now black with dirt and grime. The windows were dirty, cracked and covered in spider webs. What she saw was heart breaking. The only living things which she could see, were spiders, beetles, and other loathsome, crawling insects which scurried in every direction around her feet, hurrying into the cracks in the ground which appeared to be every where.

She placed her hand on the door and gave it a huge push to open it. It gradually gave way and opened to reveal the hideous inside of the house. She had to fight her way through the enormous spider webs which hung menacingly from every direction. The rooms were all dark and had a horrible musty smell. The rooms were very sparsely furnished with old broken furniture which was only fit for burning. The only light which entered the house was the one which she herself generated but even now after such a short time being in this place she could feel her power depleting. She sat for a moment on an old dining room chair which stood isolated in the centre of the room, then she closed her eyes and thought of the last moments that she had shared with Jamie. She imagined the sun on her face and the wind in her hair as she remembered sitting with Jamie over looking her own beautiful little home in the valley. Soon she felt a little refreshed and determined not to let this place and its all absorbing despair affect her. She had come here to help her brother and that is exactly what she intended to do.

She slowly arose from where she had been sitting and went a little further into the house. As she pushed open the next door she could see Marcus sitting in an alcove at the side of a cold empty fireplace. She spoke to him as she entered the room but there was no reaction from him. She made her way across the room and stood at the side of him. She touched his cold lifeless hand and spoke to him again. But still she got no response from him and the enormity of the task which she had taken on suddenly hit her. Her spirit sank and she could feel the power of the darkness around her increase its effect on her. But she was determined that she couldn't, wouldn't allow it to take control over her, although she knew that it would take every ounce of strength she had to fight the bleak emptiness which surrounded every thing here.

She took a step backwards and looked around the room as much as she could in this dreary light. Apart from the chair where Marcus sat, she could only see a dilapidated dust filled chaise long which sat beneath a south facing window. She removed some of the dust from the window with her hand and tried to peer through it into what should have been the flower garden. Instead of the beautiful blooms which she remembered filling the garden when on the Earth plane, all she could see now were dead stalks sticking out of the dead ground. Bugs, beetles and spiders were the only sign of life in this dreadful place. She turned and looked at Marcus sitting in the oblivion of his own despair and the sight of him made her more determined than ever to get through to him some how. Love is the strongest emotion and she would use every ounce that she possessed to help him to find within himself; the loving person who at the moment was lost to them all. She knew that only Marcus could change his situation. She hoped that her love for him could penetrate the depths of despair and despondency in which he now existed.

Annie had no idea of how long she had been with Marcus in that dark, terrible place because time has no meaning in the Spirit World. All she knew for sure was that she had lost count of the times that she had begged and pleaded with him to remember the loving young man that he had once been. She was heart broken as she looked into his blank staring eyes. She could not see even a flicker of recognition within them for her, or the memories which she had tried to recall for him. Now she became aware of the despair around her gradually eating away at her own determination. She was beginning to feel lost in the darkness which was over shadowing her whole being.

She pushed the chair on one side and sat at Marcus's feet her head resting on his hand as her warm tears of defeat flowed freely down her cheeks. Now she could only give in to the inevitability of it all. She whispered to him that she was sorry that she hadn't been able to do more to help him, but she hoped that one day he would come to realise how much she cared for him. She prayed that he would one day find the will to help himself and the desire to help others around him. She told him that this was the only way that he could move to one of the higher realms of spirit. She finally closed her eyes and allowed the forces of darkness to extinguish the last remnants of her spiritual light which had been so strong and so bright before she made the choice to enter this dreadful realm. As her warm tears flowed across his hand a small flicker of light began to shine in his eyes. His free hand reached out and touched her still head and he cried out in a sudden desperation for God to help them both. In that instant the angels of light lifted them both out of the depths of despair. They carried Marcus to a higher level in the spirit world where he would be able to help others and by doing so help himself to progress towards his goal of reaching the Summer Land.

Annie awoke to find the angels caring for her as she lay in a hospital bed. She looked around the tiny white room and realised that she was back home. But how could that be? The last thing she remembered was being in the dark and finally giving her whole being up to the darkness of despair, believing that she had failed in her quest to help her brother. She lay there quietly enjoying the peace and the warmth of love which surrounded her, but so many questions kept going through her mind.

"How did she get here?"

"Where was Marcus?"

"Was he safe?"

"Had she actually managed to help him after all?"

She didn't have to wait very long for the answers to her many questions. Nathaniel came to see her and he had a huge beaming smile on his face.

"Marcus is safe on a higher level," he told her

"He still has much work to do before he can join you on this level of the spirit world, but you have given him a chance" he said.

He explained to her that the love which had flowed in her tears and the ultimate sacrifice, which she was making, had touched his very soul. He told her that the light of her love had penetrated her brother's darkness.

"Now." he said

"Marcus would be able to love himself for who he was and later he would learn to love others too."

"The whole of the spirit realms rejoice in what you have accomplished." he told her

"Now it is time to rest before Jamie comes to take you home," he said.

Nathaniel stood at the side of her bed, made the sign of the cross and said.

"May God, bless you my child."

Then he turned away from her and was gone.

Jamie arrived soon after and took her home where she could relax in the warmth of the perpetual sunshine and see a renewed beauty in her surroundings. She turned to Jamie and said how sorry she was for putting herself into such a dangerous situation but it was something which she had got to try for her brother's sake. He put his finger to her lips and said.

"Don't apologise, I understand perfectly why you needed to try and help him."

"I am just glad that you are back safely with me."

They sat side by side, enveloped in the light of love which emanated between them.

Chapter 19

Claire returned to work two weeks after the loss of her baby. She needed to take her mind off what might have been and she needed to feel useful helping those lovely people in her charge. Although things could never be the same there since William's passing. She missed his smiling face and his silly jokes but she knew that life had to go on. Every one welcomed her back to work and Helena passed on every one's condolences at the loss of the child which she had been carrying. She thanked them all and then continued with her duties as usual. The following weeks flew by quite uneventfully for which every one was extremely grateful.

Claire loved Thursday afternoons when the residents had their usual sing along. Helena had continued to play the piano for them even though she missed William singing at her side. As she walked into the community room Claire saw Helena sitting in her usual place at the piano and the sing along was in full swing. There were happy smiling faces all around the room until Helena suddenly stopped playing and a silence descended into the room. Helena's hands were shaking and her face turned ashen white. Claire and her co-worker, Pat helped Helena into a wheel chair and took her to her room. They placed her on top of her bed and Claire's heart skipped a beat.

"Oh!"

"No"

"Not again"

Claire sobbed as she watched the life slip quickly away from Helena.

As she stood helplessly at the side of the bed Claire became aware of a shiny silver chord breaking away from Helena's body as she breathed her last. At the same time she saw two bright orbs of light enter the room. They hovered over the body for a moment or two and then one of them disappeared without trace. Claire knew at that moment that Wilfred had come to collect his beloved wife. The other orb floated around the room and hovered at her side, then she felt the familiar touch of Annie's hand upon hers and she realised that her friend had come to give her support and to let her know that all would be well with Helena.

This was the first time that Claire had witnessed with her own eyes the spirit leaving a person's physical body. She had seen beings from the spirit world and she felt in awe of their beauty. She felt a wonderful sense of peace within her mind. She felt no sadness, only joy in the knowledge that Helena and her husband were now reunited in spirit. Claire finished her shift and went home to Richard with many mixed emotions going round and around in her head. She couldn't wait to tell Richard what she had witnessed that afternoon. She was still having difficulty believing what she had seen with her own eyes.

That evening as Claire and Richard sat curled up together on the settee she told him that she was thinking of resigning from her job. She had seen her two favourite residents die and she didn't think that she could face the though of losing any more. She told him that she was beginning to feel tired now and all she wanted was to stay at home and take care of the house and him. They were now in a comfortable financial position and it wasn't necessary for her to go out to work any more. She wanted the time to enjoy the home that they had both worked so hard for. She would miss the busy routine that she had become accustomed to but now she felt the need to slow down a little bit and enjoy life. Richard was very happy to support her decision because now they would be able to spend more quality time together.

Claire enjoyed her new lifestyle especially in a morning when Richard brought her a cup of tea to bed before he rushed of to work at the hospital. She spent the first couple of months redecorating inside the house, buying new carpets and curtains. The only room in the house that didn't get a make over was the nursery. She freshened the room up with a new coat of paint but every thing else was left as it had always been. The teddies were still lined up in the cot, and the mobiles still hung above it. Even after all these years she couldn't bring herself to change anything in that room. It was still referred to as Michael Paul's room but as she looked around she couldn't help the longing which ached within her constantly. For Richard's sake as much as her own she had slowly come to terms with everything that had happened to them. It was only very occasionally when she was alone, that she would allow her maternal longings to come to the forefront and for a few moments she would be lost in her own thoughts and longings.

But now she was strong enough to have these feelings and then push them to the back of her mind in total acceptance of the fate that life had dealt her.

Annie had often heard Claire's thoughts and had quite often stood beside her in Michael Paul's room. She had felt Claire's pain and had so often wished that she could do some thing to help her young friend but for now all she could do was try and support her from the spirit side of life. She would always watch over them both because the bond of love which bound her to them on the Earth plane would never be broken.

With the extra time on her hands Claire would often take an afternoon stroll to the cemetery. She enjoyed the peace and quiet which she found there and of course she felt closer to her son during those visits. It was during one of these visits that she met Marion. She was kneeling down re-arranging the flowers on Michael Paul's grave when she heard a soft sobbing coming from behind her. She listened for a few moments and she recognised the depth of grief which she could hear in those sobs. She turned and looked around to see if she could make out where the sobs were coming from. She turned a little to the right and saw a young woman tenderly touching a shiny white headstone, which looked as though it was at the head of a child's grave. Claire decided to try and talk to the young woman who she thought was obviously the child's mother. As she got closer the young woman turned to look at Claire. The pallor of her skin made her red swollen eyes stand out.

Claire stood at her side and exclaimed in shock as she read not one but two children's names on the headstone.

"They were twins," the young woman explained to Claire.

She also told her that the babies, twin girls, were still born.

She had been involved in a car accident at eight months and her beautiful baby girls were born shortly afterwards. She couldn't even attend the funeral service because she was in a coma in hospital for a few weeks after the accident. Her husband David had arranged everything and he had attended the service on his own. She said that she found it difficult to come to terms with and even more difficult to forgive herself, although the accident hadn't been her fault she still felt guilty. She told Claire that her husband had been her rock. He had supported her through every thing and if it wasn't for his strength, she didn't think that she could have carried on living.

Claire gave her what few words of comfort that she could while thinking how insignificant they sounded. As they stood at the graveside it began raining heavily and Claire suggested that they shelter in the church porch way which as only a few yards in front of them.

"There is a seat in there where we can sit until the rain stops,"

Claire explained as they dashed out of the rain which was now coming down in sheets.

As they sat there Claire introduced herself to her companion and the young woman said that her name was Marion.

"Today is the first day that I have visited my babies by myself," she explained.

"I had an uncontrollable urge which wouldn't go away."

"I needed to tell my girls that I was so sorry about what had happened," she said.

The two women talked for about an hour and they found that they had a lot in common with their likes and dislikes. Marion said that she was so grateful to have some one to talk to at last who understood what she was feeling inside. She explained that her family and friends were very supportive but they had no idea of what she was feeling and the thoughts which were constantly going through her head. Claire told her that she would be there for her when ever she wanted to talk about anything at all. If she could help in any way she would she assured her. She asked Marion where she lived and was amazed to discover that they both lived in the same street. Marion told her that she and her husband David had moved into number one twelve months previously but they had not yet had chance to get to know any of their neighbours and she was feeling very isolated and very vulnerable at the moment. Claire told her that she lived at number ninety and that she was welcome to call at her house any time.

"Who knows, maybe we were meant to meet here today?" Claire said to her.

"Maybe we were."

Marion replied with just a hint of a smile breaking out at the corners of her mouth.

The rain finally stopped and the two women both said, "Goodbye" to their respective children and left the cemetery together.

"It really has been wonderful to have someone to talk to, who understands what I am going through," Marion told Claire.

"David has been so caring towards me but he doesn't really understand how I feel inside," she said.

During the next few weeks and months a special bond of friendship grew between the women. They became inseparable and Claire jokingly said to Richard that she felt more like a big sister to Marion rather than just being a friend. She also told him that she had often wondered whether it had been a coincidence that they had met that day, or had their meeting been engineered by an unseen friend?

"I don't suppose we shall ever know for sure," he said lazily, as he put his arm around her waist, pulled her to him and kissed her tenderly on the lips.

She loved her husband dearly but how could she tell him that her mind and body still ached for the touch, the sensation of holding her own child in her arms. She was aware of the decision that they had both made so many years ago. But her heart was ruling her head and the thought of her fortieth birthday only being two years away was heightening the feelings that she was having. She could feel her body clock ticking away and she had no control over it. However, she kept her thoughts away from her husband because she didn't want to place him in a difficult situation. She didn't want him to see the pain which she suffered inside on a daily basis. She was sure that it would be too much for him to bear.

Chapter 20

Thoughts are living things and Annie had listened to Claire's so many times as they had winged their way to the higher realms of life. She knew the pain which Claire carried in her heart and she was determined to do whatever it took to help her friend. Somehow she would replace the deep sorrow with joy. Although it as never spoken of, she knew and understood every feeling and emotion that Claire experienced. She understood the longing which Claire had of wanting a child of her own, to hold in her arms and to love. If there was a way to help her friend she would find it but first she needed to discuss her thoughts with Jamie.

As they sat in their beautiful garden enjoying the sweet perfume of the flowers and watching the honey bees and butterflies flit from flower to flower Annie turned to Jamie and told him that there was something that she wished to discuss with him. He turned to look at her with the sweetest smile playing around his lips.

"I have known for some time what is in your heart and how you wish to help Claire," he said to her, with love and admiration shining in his eyes.

"How could I begin to help her?" She asked him.

"We need to talk to Nathaniel," he told her.

"He will know what to do."

They found Nathaniel in the Halls of Learning writing the names of the new arrivals into the Book of Souls. When he had finished writing he turned to Annie and Jamie with a knowing look on his face. He told them that he had known for a long time what was in Annie's heart and that he also knew that Jamie had made the decision to follow her. He understood the reasons why she wanted to help her friend and why Jamie couldn't stay in the spirit world without his soul mate. He said that he would do what was necessary to help them with their decisions. He explained that they would have to go before the Committee of Elders to obtain their permission to return to the earth plane as new spirit souls. He also explained to them that it wasn't a decision to be taken lightly because as new souls, they would lose all memory of themselves and what they were now and the love which they have for each other. He told them that they would begin life anew and that they would make a whole new existence for themselves. He suggested that they go away and think about what he had said and take time to realise the consequences for themselves.

They thanked Nathaniel for the help and advice which he had offered to them but they both knew exactly what was involved and they were sure, that they wanted to continue with this course of action. He watched them as they left the Halls of Learning and he felt a twinge of sadness because he knew that they would both be sadly missed by all in the Spirit World. But they had made their choice and he would do every thing possible to help them.

They didn't have to wait long before they were summoned into the council chamber to face the Committee of Elders. As they entered the room Annie froze in her tracks with trepidation. She looked around her and saw that the rows of seats were now full. This time there weren't just five Elders in front of where they would be standing. There were faces peering down onto them from all directions. But their decision was made and they would stand together, side by side, to state their case for wanting to return to a life on the Earth Plane. They were strong in their faith in each other and they knew that even another life time would not separate them. They knew that, one day, they would find each other again. They would fight against all the odds to be together again and they were prepared for the gamble which they would have to over come to have the material existence for which they both craved.

Jamie pleaded their case of returning to the Earth Plane to the Elders. He spoke with such passion about the bond of love which held both he and Annie to those on the Earth Plane, who needed this act of kindness from them. He explained that their decision was freely made out of love for others. He also told the committee that this wasn't an act of self indulgence for himself and Annie. Indeed, it was a gift which they both wanted to give to people who they considered to be very special.

He told the Committee members that in his mind, they were people who deserved to know the love of parenthood to its fullest extent.

The Elders and Committee listened with great care to what Jamie was saying to them. They confirmed their wishes with them both, to make sure that they were fully aware of how their decision would affect them and that once the Committee had agreed there would be no going back on their decision. They both acknowledged that they fully understood what had been said but they had no intention of changing their minds. With the conditions laid out in front of them both, their final decision was made and the Committee gave their blessing and their permission for Annie and Jamie to return to the Earth Plane as new spirit souls. They both left the committee room with very mixed emotions. They knew that they had made the right choice but at the same time there was an element of fear and excitement of taking their transition from the Spirit World, to live another life on Earth.

Chapter 21

Blissfully unaware of the preparations which had been made and executed in the Spirit World, Richard was making preparations of his own. Next year would be Claire's fortieth birthday and he wanted to do something very special for her, especially as he was having growing concerns about her health. She was looking tired and pale most days lately but if he approached the subject she would merely smile at him and put her condition down to her age.

"Well, I am nearly forty," she would joke with him and then dismiss the subject.

Richard accepted her explanation each time but it didn't stop him worrying, so the next time that he saw Wendy at work, he took her on one side and asked her to call in and see Claire. He said that he would value her opinion. Wendy was only too pleased to do as he asked. She said that she was due to visit Claire any way the following Tuesday and then she would let him know what she thought.

Tuesday afternoon arrived and Wendy found Claire working in the front garden.

"I am pleased to see you," Claire said to her.

"It gives me a good excuse for putting my feet up for a few minutes,," she laughed.

"You go and sit down while I make us a cup of tea" Wendy told her.

Wendy went into the kitchen while Claire went into the garden at the rear of the house. The garden which Richard had designed and built for her was her pride and joy. It reflected the love which he had put into it for her with its neatly trimmed lawns and borders full of colour from summer flowering plants. Her favourite spot was the summer house which he built at the top of the garden. It was surrounded by the most fragrant orange blossom trees, and their perfume wafted all through the garden.

She sat in the summer house and watched Wendy as she carried the tea tray towards her. The two women sat in silence for a moment or two as they enjoyed the vista in front of them. Wendy looked at Claire and remarked at how tired she was looking and asked her how she was feeling.

"I want the truth from you, I don't want to hear one of your usual glib answers," she said to her friend.

Claire looked at her and gave a small sigh of relief.

"I am so pleased to have some one to talk to other than Richard," she told Wendy.

"I haven't been feeling too good just lately" she admitted to her friend.

She told her that Richard had been asking after her health recently but she had dismissed his questions because she didn't want to worry him. She admitted that she was becoming concerned for herself, but thought that it may be the onset of the menopause. She told Wendy that she had missed her periods for two months so she thought that it was the most obvious option.

Wendy suggested that she made an appointment to see her GP and if she wanted some company, she would go with her. Claire said that she would be very grateful of the company. She said that she would have asked Marion to accompany her but she had to go to Essex to care for her mother who was not well and she didn't know when she would be back at home. Claire made the appointment for the following week and Wendy made arrangements at work to have the time off to go with her. When Wendy saw Richard she told him that she wasn't unduly worried about Claire but she did feel that a visit to her GP was called for. She assured him that she didn't feel that there was anything for him to worry too much about. Silently she thought to herself that she had a very good idea what was wrong with Claire but at this moment in time she didn't want to share her thoughts with him.

'What if I am totally wrong with what I am thinking?' she thought to herself, so she decided to keep her thoughts to herself.

A week later the two women entered the doctor's surgery. He was one of the old school sitting behind his desk with his glasses half way down his nose. He looked over the top of them when he spoke, but he had kind eyes and a soothing manner and put Claire at ease immediately. She explained to him how she had been feeling lately and said that recently she had become quite nauseous, most of the time.

"Please go behind the curtain and get onto the bed so that I can examine you," he said.

When he had finished he went to his desk, sat down and waited for Claire to join him when she was ready.

She sat nervously in front of him waiting for his diagnosis. He looked at her with a smile on his face and said.

"I hope that you are ready for a very pleasant piece of news".

He assured her that her condition was nothing to do with her age what so ever. He looked her straight in the eyes from over the top of his glasses and said.

"Knowing your past history I didn't expect to ever again tell you this, but I am telling you now, that you are three months pregnant."

Claire looked at him feeling quite stunned for a few moments until the full realisation of what had been said struck home to her. She was three months pregnant. Her GP said that he would make all of the arrangements for her to visit the antenatal clinic.

"Of course due to your age and medical history you will be closely monitored" he assured her.

He reached over the desk and touched her hand and whispered his congratulations. She thanked the Doctor and walked out of the surgery in a daze. She barely remembered the journey home as her mind was in turmoil; so many emotions flooded her brain. Thank goodness Wendy was with her because being told that she was pregnant was the last thing which she expected to hear.

Richard came home to find her in tears. What had the doctor told her?

"Claire!" he said.

"What is wrong?"

There were so many tears that he expected to hear some dreadful news. He certainly wasn't prepared for what she was about to tell him. She looked at him through the tears slipping down her face and told him to sit down next to her.

"It's a miracle" she sobbed and laughed all at the same time.

"I am three months pregnant"

"Pregnant, but I thought....", she put her hand up to his lips.

"I know what you are going to say," she said

"But it's true, I am PREGNANT!" she shouted

They sat and hugged each other and their tears of joy mingled together.

"I can't believe it," he said

"It's a miracle.,"

When he had got over the shock, he told her that he had been planning a surprise trip to Paris for her birthday but she had out done him with her own surprise. He had better cancel the trip as soon as possible.

"I think that you had better" she said.

"I should be having the baby for my birthday present if my calculations are correct," she laughingly told him.

The months slipped by quickly and her health improved as the pregnancy progressed in fact Richard often told her that she looked stunning. Pregnancy was suiting her. The scans and examinations came and went and they discovered that she was carrying a little girl so Richard busied himself redecorating the nursery. All of the blue paint and other old fixtures had been replaced with a pretty soft pink colour. He put up new shelves and Claire lovingly lined up all of Michael Paul's teddies and other soft toys. The old cot was replaced by a new crib with pretty pink satin drapes and eiderdown. How pretty it all looked she thought as she stood in the centre of the room admiring Richard's handy work. As she stood there she heard some one knocking on the back door and then she heard a familiar voice shouting to her. It was Marion. She must have finally come home from her mother's Claire thought as she hurried down the stairs towards the kitchen where Marion was sitting at the table.

As Claire entered the kitchen Marion stood up and both women stared at one another in disbelief. They were both pregnant!

Claire put the kettle on to make a cup of tea before they settled down to catch up on what had been happening.

Marion said that she had found out that she was pregnant two weeks after she had gone to care for her mother, who incidentally was doing fine now.

"What date have you been given?" She asked Claire.

"The fourth of April, my birthday" she replied.

"And you?"

"What date have you been given?

"The thirtieth of March," she said as she patted the huge bump in front of her.

They sat drinking tea and catching up for the next two hours. They both said that they were nervous of telling the other about their condition because they hadn't wanted to hurt each other's feelings. Then they looked at one another and had a good laugh about every thing.

"Life can play some funny tricks on us," Claire said to her friend.

"I still can't believe that we are both due to have our babies so close together, it's quite unbelievable." they both agreed.

Marion looked at her watch, it was three thirty.

"I had better go home and start preparing David's evening meal" she said to her friend.

The two women stood up and each hugged the other as well as they could with two large bumps between them.

"See you tomorrow," Marion shouted as she waddled down the path towards the pavement on her way home.

Claire was overjoyed and rather overwhelmed to think that they were both pregnant and their babies were due so close together. She said to Richard that, "It felt as though some one unseen had manipulated the situation."

Claire and Marion went shopping together, went to antenatal classes together and best of all they shared their joy and excitement at their impending births. Marion took Claire to see the new nursery all decked out in blue. She and David were going to have a son.

The last few weeks dragged by too slowly for both women but eventually the end of March arrived, then it was the beginning of April and there was still no sign of Marion's son wanting to arrive. They both started counting the days down in April until the early hours of the third, when Marion was admitted into the maternity unit. She was followed by Claire during the middle of the afternoon on the same day. Each of them had been placed in a small side room so neither knew that the other was there.

The following day they were taken onto the recovery ward and to their amazement their beds were placed side by side. Both had been delivered safely and each one was so proud of their beautiful baby. Each a special gift from God. Shortly afterwards the two babies were brought onto the ward and placed into their mother's arms. Marion turned to Claire and showed her, her son.

"What are you going to call him?" asked Claire

"Samuel David," she replied.

"Samuel is a family name."

"David's father is called Samuel but I think that it suits this little man here," she said with a huge beaming smile on her face.

"I think that you are quite right," said Claire as she admired the precious bundle in her friend's arms.

"What are you naming your little girl?" Marion enquired.

"We are not sure at the moment," said Claire.

"I am waiting for Richard to come back before we make the final decision," she explained.

The two women then placed their children back into their cribs and settled down for a well deserved rest. Marion was soon asleep but Claire was restlessly drifting in and out of sleep. She was finding it difficult to take her eyes off her baby and to allow herself to relax into a state of sleep. Finally she closed her eyes but instead of the calming darkness of sleep, she became aware of a bright light at the side of her bed. She looked into the light and saw her beloved son standing next to her bed. He had the sweetest of smiles on his face which melted any feeling of fear which she may have had. He whispered to his mother that his sister was perfect and that she had come to the Earth to stay. He assured his mother that she had no reason to fear anything happening to his sister. They would live a long and happy life together as a family. He also told her that now was the time for him to begin his work in the Spirit World and he would not visit her and his father on a regular basis any more. He said that, he was now needed else where but he would always be in their hearts so he would never be very far from them.

Claire silently said, "Goodbye" to her son and watched as he placed a kiss on the baby's head before he disappeared from her view. She then drifted into a deep, contented sleep knowing that their future happiness as a family was secure. Richard was the first one through the door at visiting time armed with a huge bouquet for Claire and an enormous pink rabbit for his daughter. As they sat talking Claire told him of the visit she'd had from Michael Paul and they thanked God together for the most precious of all gifts which He had given to them.

"What are we going to call her?" Claire asked him.

"I have been thinking of Lauren Michelle," she told him.

He agreed, he liked the names very much and as he picked his daughter up he whispered.

"Lauren Michelle, Mummy and Daddy love you very much."

He carried her to the window to show the world their beautiful little daughter and to quietly say thank you to God for her safe delivery. At last they knew, in their heart of hearts, that they had a future together as a happy loving family.

Chapter 22

C laire looked across the kitchen table at her husband. He was still the most handsome man she knew. His dark hair was almost white now and he had lately grown a moustache which she thought made him look even more distinguished. How she loved to look at his handsome face. He leaned across the table and lovingly touched her out stretched hand.

"I love you." He said in a low seductive voice and "I can't imagine my life without you."

She smiled and whispered. "I love you too.".

A few moments later they heard the clip clop of heels coming towards the kitchen doorway, they looked across the kitchen to see Lauren standing there. They both, stared at her in disbelief, gone was their tom boy daughter and in her place stood a beautiful young woman all dressed up ready for the School Prom. Her long blonde curly hair hung down her back like a shining water fall. Her full length dress of midnight blue highlighted the pale blue of her eyes.

"You look stunning," her parents said in unison. "Is Samuel coming to pick you up?" her mother asked with a twinkle in her eyes.

"He should be here in about five minutes," she replied. "And by the way, don't get any ideas, he is my best friend and I don't want anything spoiling that," she said, lovingly chiding her mother. The door bell rang and soon Samuel was standing in the kitchen with them.

"My, don't you look smart?" Claire said as she gave him a very approving smile.

"What has happened to the jeans and tee shirt?"

He just laughed with her and said that he thought that he had better dress up tonight or Lauren would never forgive him. He handed Lauren the corsage which he had been holding and waited while her mother fixed it onto her dress for her. She gave him a quick peck on the cheek and then they went on their way to the prom, giggling between them as usual.

Claire turned to her husband and said. "I know that they have always been friends but there is something about their friendship which makes me feel that it should be a lot more." "They are like two sides of the same coin."

Her husband agreed with her, sighed and then went to get a bottle of their favourite wine. He took her hand and led her into the sitting room.

"Make yourself comfortable and we can sit here with our wine and relax for a pleasant change," he told her.

They curled up on the sofa together silently embracing the love and contentment which flowed between them. Life had had its cruel moments but its adversities had given them a bond of love which nothing and no-one could ever break. Claire gave a gentle sigh and said, "I wish that Annie was still here so that she could have seen our beautiful Lauren this evening."

"It is strange how we both stopped being aware of her presence around us as soon as I became pregnant." Claire remarked.

"I thought that myself," said Richard. "But I also thought that it might be because she knew that everything was going to be alright for us." "Annie always did have a knack of knowing things about us that no-one else did."

"It was as if she had a sixth sense where we were concerned," he said with a slight hint of sadness in his voice. "I must confess that I have missed being aware of her presence around us in times of need," he said. "I remember praying for Annie to help us, when Lauren was about five years old and we thought that we had lost her." "Do you remember that dreadful day?" He asked.

"Over the years I have often thought about that Sunday afternoon." Claire said to her husband. "One minute she was happily playing in the garden and the next minute she had disappeared." "We searched everywhere for her, through the house, in the garden shed and the summer house." "We called her name and ran up and down the road looking for her but she was nowhere to be seen." "Even old Mr Wilkins next door helped us search for her." "We were frantic with worry and what a relief when he called over the garden fence to say that he had found her," she recalled.

They couldn't help but laugh when they remembered seeing Lauren curled up asleep in the dog kennel with Sandy, Mr Wilkins' dog. Lauren had woken up oblivious of the panic which she had caused her parents. She had been playing with Sandy and when he lay down she just lay down with him and went to sleep. Her parents hugged her and her mother held her close and told her never to go to play anywhere outside of the garden without telling her first. Lauren had agreed and then had gone skipping back home as if nothing had happened. Claire and Richard thanked Mr Wilkins and followed their daughter home.

Claire and Richard each became lost in their own thoughts of their darling daughter for a short time. There were so many memories of the past while Lauren was growing up. She had always been a lively little girl and always had a very strong will. She was never a deliberately naughty child but because she had a strong self belief she could never see the danger in anything she did and she usually managed to talk Samuel into being her accomplice. Richard turned to his wife and asked her if she could remember the time that they had taken the children to the circus.

"Oh! I remember," said Claire. "It was a lovely sunny day and the children were so excited at seeing all of the wild animals." "I remember that Samuel wanted to see the lions and tigers, but Lauren was more interested in the trapeze artists and clowns."

"She always loved dressing up in your old dresses and clonking around in your high heels," Richard remembered fondly.

They had been seated on the front row and Lauren was jumping up and down in her seat when the clowns appeared in the ring. When Buster, the lead clown had a bucket of water in his hand and was about to throw it over the audience, Lauren was squealing with excitement. She wanted to get the bucket and throw it over the people herself. It wasn't long before she caught Buster's eye and he asked Claire and Richard if their little girl could join them in the ring.

"Can I please Mommy?" Lauren had begged.

"Yes, you can." Her mother had agreed with a huge smile on her face.

Buster quickly put some make-up and a huge red nose on her before getting a large straw hat with a flower on the side which squirted water when she pressed a rubber ball which she held in her hand. She had a wonderful time, squirting water all over all of the clowns. But best of all was when she ran in front of her parents and Samuel and squirted water all over them. It was great fun. One of the other clowns gave her a blow-up beach ball to throw at the sea lion which was sitting on his platform waiting to catch the ball on the end of his nose. Lauren had to throw the ball a number of times before the sea lion caught it but eventually she had got it just right and he caught it every time. The animal was clapping its flippers and making a very loud honking noise which made Lauren put her hands over her ears. Soon it was time for her to take her seat and watch the rest of the show. How she had enjoyed herself.

When the show had finished and everyone was leaving to go home, Buster went to Claire and Richard and asked if they would like to have a guided tour around the back of the circus where only the circus folk are allowed to go. They would be delighted they assured him. Lauren and Samuel didn't need asking twice, they each grabbed one of Buster's hands and almost dragged him out of the Big Top. Their first stop was by a huge cage where the two Bengal tigers lived. Samuel wanted to know everything about them. "Where did they come from?" "What did they eat?" "How old were they?" "What were their names?" "Slow down young man," said Buster laughingly. "I will answer all of your questions in a moment but first I would like to get out of my costume and take this make-up off my face." He handed the children back to

Claire and Richard and asked if they would like to sit in his trailer while he got changed. They said that they would and he led them to the seating area while he went to the other end of the trailer and closed the door behind him. The children were mesmerised by the photographs and posters hanging on the walls. There was even a chart showing how to apply the clowns make up together with dozens of different faces.

"Wow," said Samuel. "I didn't know that there were so many."

A short while later Buster re-appeared looking quite normal and the children hardly recognised him for the man that went into the changing room. He was a tall young man of about 30 years of age with ginger hair and a dashing smile which showed off his set of perfect white teeth. "Are we all ready then?" he asked the children with outstretched hands.

"You bet we are," they said in unison. Both children held an outstretched hand and giggled with excitement.

"Off we go then," he said as he led them out of his trailer and began their journey around the all of the circus animals and all of the entertainers. The time flew by and soon it was time to say, "Goodbye" to their new friend. Richard thanked him for making such a memorable time for all of them and promised to take the children back again next time that the circus was in town. The children didn't stop talking all of the way home. It had been such an incredible experience for them. Claire and Richard couldn't help smiling as they remembered all of the circus games that the children had played for weeks after their adventure. It was only a few weeks after this that Samuel told Claire, that when he grew up he was going to become a vet and work with lions and tigers. Claire smiled at him and told him that he would probably change his mind when he got older but Samuel looked her straight in the eye and said that he would never change his mind. He was adamant that he would one day become a wild life Veterinary Surgeon. She could see a steely determination in his face and told him that she thought that it was a wonderful idea and she wished him all the luck in the world.

Richard glanced at the clock as it struck midnight.

"Lauren should be home soon," he said sleepily to his wife.

"I think that it is time that we went to bed," Claire said as she stifled a yawn.

"You go on up," he said. "I will follow you up in a few minutes." "I want to check that the doors and windows are locked before I come up."

As he approached the front door it burst open, followed by a peel of laughter as Lauren and Samuel walked into the house. Lauren kissed her father on the cheek as she went past him almost dragging Samuel with her as she went into the lounge.

"Your mother and I are going to bed now so don't make too much noise and don't stay up too late." He told her as he wished them both, "Goodnight."

"You can tell us all about it tomorrow," he told her as he turned to make his way upstairs to the waiting arms of his loving wife.

Chapter 23

The sun shone through the windows as they all sat around the kitchen table drinking coffee and chatting about the previous evening. Lauren told her parents all about the wonderful time that she had had at the school prom. The school hall had been decked out with banners wishing all of the student's Good Luck and Best Wishes for their futures. The walls and ceilings had coloured fairy lights draped everywhere and there was even a disco ball hanging from the centre of the ceiling. The buffet table ran the whole length of the hall and was crammed with all sorts of delicacies. The school had also hired a local rock band to play for them who were absolutely brilliant she told her parents. "The night couldn't have been any better," she told them. Quite suddenly her happy go lucky mood changed to that of sadness as she recalled her conversation with Samuel the evening before. He had reminded her that tomorrow he was leaving for Veterinary College.

Her mother saw the wistful look in her eyes and guessed that her change of mood had something to do with Samuel.

"When does Samuel go to Veterinary College?" her mother asked her.

"Tomorrow," said Lauren with a hint of sorrow in her voice.

"I think that the reality of him going has just hit me," she said. "I have known about it for a long time but now that the time is nearly here I am realising how much I am going to miss him." "I guess life won't be the same without him here, it will be as if a part of me is missing." She said as her eyes filled with moisture.

Her mother put her loving arms around her shoulders and gently reminded her that soon she would be going off to University. "Life moves on, things change and that is all part of growing up," she lovingly whispered in her daughter's ear.

"Have you and Samuel got anything planned for today?" she asked.

"Yes," she said jumping up from the table.

"We are having a day shopping because we both need things to take with us, so we thought that we would go together."

"When we have finished Samuel is treating me to a meal at that new Italian restaurant in town." She told her mother with a big beaming smile on her face.

Lauren walked down the hallway towards the front door, reached for her coat off the hook, opened the front door as she shouted, "Goodbye," to her mother and was gone.

Claire reached for the kettle and put it on to boil. She was ready for a coffee and a sit down while she contemplated the future without the two children being constantly around her. Part of her felt excitement for them as they started out on their life's journey but at the same time part of her felt devastated at the thought of losing them. Inwardly she chided herself for being so silly, after all her baby had to grow up sometime and she was so proud of the young woman that Lauren had become. She finished drinking her coffee, put her silly thoughts behind her and made a start on the housework.

Hours later and her housework finished she sat with her feet up on the sofa when she heard the familiar sound of giggling as Lauren and Samuel came rushing in. They were constantly none stop chatter between themselves. Quite suddenly their happy mood changed as Samuel looked at the clock and realised that it was almost time to make his way home. They both knew that this was the last day that they would be together as happy carefree young people, because tomorrow was the beginning of their new lives without each other's company. Samuel said, "Goodbye" to Claire and asked her to pass on his regards to Richard for him; he was going to miss them both very much. They were his second family he told Claire as he put his arms around her. gave her a kiss on the cheek and thanked her for always being there for him.

Claire wiped the tears away from her eyes as she walked out into the garden for a few moments while Samuel said his farewell to Lauren. They hugged each other for a few moments and promised that they would keep in touch as often as possible. We can always text or use Skype to keep in touch they told one another through the tears. A few moments later Lauren watched as Samuel walked up the road towards his home. She slowly closed the door, walked into the sitting room and sank into the sofa. Life was going to be very different from now on and she suddenly felt so alone. It was as if she had watched part of herself walking up that road and out of her life for the foreseeable future. She had always known that this day would arrive but she hadn't realised how painful it would be for her. She wondered whether Samuel was feeling the same way about missing her.

The following morning Lauren was up bright and early to wave goodbye to Samuel as he embarked on his journey to his new life in the Veterinary world. His parents stood at her side as they watched the taxi drive away, taking their son to the train station where he would catch the train to Hampshire. They had so much pride showing in their faces as his mother recalled that he hadn't wanted them to go with him. He was a man now and he wanted to make this journey alone. He also explained that he had wanted his last mental picture of them all to be where he had only known happiness; he was taking so many happy memories with him he assured them all. When the car had disappeared, Marion put a hand on Lauren's shoulder lovingly and whispered in her ear,

"We are still here for you when you want us."

Lauren hugged them both and then made her way back home to her parents who were waiting for her with a hot cup of tea.

"I will get breakfast for us in a moment," her mother told her.

"And then we will have to discuss your arrangements for University, because time is getting very short."

"You have only got another week and then you will be gone." "I don't know what your dad and I will do when you are gone, the house will be so quiet," her mother told her with a hint of sadness in her voice.

Lauren hugged her mother as if to reassure her but she knew that life would never be the same again. It was time now for her and Samuel to make their own mark, their own way in life even if it did feel as if they were going in opposite directions. Lauren had been accepted into Oxford University where she was going to read Languages and Geology. She had been an "A" level student in French and German at school and she wanted to travel the world either as an Interpreter or as a Geologist. Her interest in Geology had developed from metal detecting with her father whenever he had a weekend to spare.

The following week flew by as Lauren made her final preparations for University. Her bags were packed together with books and stationary which she would need. She was beginning to feel very nervous and at the same time very excited about the future. At that moment her phone started beeping, it was Samuel texting to wish her luck and to say that he had settled in to his rooms at college. He sounded as if he was having a ball. His room-mate was called Neil and they got on very well together and he was really looking forward to the next five years.

Chapter 24

It was a bright Sunday morning when Marion and David said, "Goodbye," to Claire, Richard and Lauren as they set off for Oxford. The atmosphere in the car was very subdued as they made the two hour journey as each of them was deep in their own thoughts. Claire and Richard were both thinking about the headstrong yet loving daughter that they were so proud of and were going to miss so much. Lauren was thinking of all the happy times she had had as a child, there was so much to think of. Her parents had always been very hands on and had given so much of themselves to her throughout her childhood. She was remembering the time that her father had bought a metal detector and they had taken Samuel with them spending hours looking for lost treasures. She realised how lucky she had been because she only had happy memories and that was all thanks to her wonderful parents.

At last they arrived, what an impressive vista laid before them. What magnificent sand stone buildings surrounded them as they stood transfixed for a few moments. Half an hour later they were standing in the middle of the room which was to become Lauren's home for the next three years. There were two single beds, one at each side of the room. A small bedside cupboard stood at the side of each bed. Under the window stood two small desks, with room enough for a laptop and printer. The opposite wall held two single built in wardrobes with just enough room for a small dressing table for each occupant. The room was already occupied when she arrived so she put her things away in the empty drawers and wardrobe on the right hand side of the room. When they arrived Claire had noticed a vending machine further up the corridor from Lauren's room, so she told them that she was going to get them all a cup of coffee before she and Richard had to leave. They were soon holding a nice hot cup of coffee whilst sitting on the bed chatting about anything and everything. For a short while they were all trying to avoid the inevitable goodbye which was very close at hand now.

Half an hour later Lauren was stood at the side of the car saying, "Goodbye," to her parents. Both she and her mother were trying to hide the tears which were welling up in their eyes. They put on a happy face to hide the sudden loneliness which was already beginning to creep into their hearts. Soon her parents were out of sight and Lauren made her way back to her room. Slowly she took out of her bag the few personal items which she had brought. On the dressing table taking pride of place was her favourite photograph of her parents and Samuel. She had taken it two years previously when the orange blossom was in full bloom in front of the summer house her father had built for her mother so many years ago. It was still her favourite place in the garden because it held so many special memories for her. She had sat there with Marion many times over the years and watched their children as they played and as they grew from babies into strong healthy children and latterly as young adults.

When she arrived back at her room she heard the sound of music and a young woman singing to the words of the song. Lauren lightly knocked on the door and entered. The young woman swung around to see who was there and gave Lauren a big friendly smile.

"Hello," she said.

"You don't need to knock, this is your room as well as mine," she said extending a friendly hand towards Lauren. "My name is Joanne and you must be Lauren."

"I was wondering when you would get here," she said.

Lauren took her hand and said. "Hello Joanne it's lovely to meet you I was wondering who I would be sharing with."

The girls hit it off immediately and Joanne was soon giving Lauren a tour of the University campus.

"Are you hungry?" Joanne asked.

"Starving," Lauren replied.

"Come on then," she replied. "I know of a lovely little pub quite close to here where we can get a meal at reasonable prices."

The pub was quite crowded when the girls got there and there seemed to be a lot of people that Joanne knew. Lauren was made to feel at ease straight away and was soon chatting away to what was soon to become a huge crowd of new friends. The two girls didn't have to wait very long for a table to become vacant for their meal. Both girls had a minted lamb shank with creamed potatoes and vegetables.

"That was delicious," Lauren said, as she scraped the last bit of potato from her plate.

"What are we having for pudding?" she asked as she scanned the sweet Menu.

"The Death by Chocolate looks good," she told Joanne with an impish smile on her face.

"I couldn't agree more," said Joanne as she beckoned the waiter over and ordered two, Death by Chocolates. The girls finished their puddings in silence but when they had finished eating, they both agreed that they couldn't eat another mouth full. They paid the bill and said, "Goodnight," to their friends in the pub and took a steady walk back to their room.

The girls sat on the side of their beds facing each other across the room. "I didn't expect my first day here to be so eventful." Lauren confided in Joanne.

"I am not sure what I expected but it certainly wasn't such a pleasant end to the day."

A short while later her phone rang and it was her mother letting her know that they had got home safely and they hoped that she was alright. She told her mother that she had had a lovely evening and that she had met a lot of new friends. She assured her mother that she was going to be alright and that she was not to worry about her any more. Claire wished her daughter, "Goodnight," told her she loved her and that she would pass the good news on to her father. Lauren said, "Goodnight" to her mother and told her. she loved her too before she put the phone down.

"Parents!" said Lauren to Joanne in a joking sort of way.

"It must be lovely to be so close to your parents?" Joanne said in a questioning sort of way. "My parents left me to find my own way here when I arrived last year," she told her new friend.

"Why was that, if you don't mind my asking?" said Lauren feeling very sorry for the sad looking girl who sat in front of her.

"Oh! My parents had just split up and my mother was going away to Italy with her new man," Joanne said, with more than a hint of sadness in her voice. Lauren commiserated with her new friend and left the girl deep in her own thoughts. Lauren broke the ensuing silence by saying that she was going to get ready for bed. A short time later she was texting Samuel to wish him good night and to let him know that she had happily settled in to her new- room and was looking forward to beginning her studies the next day. He texted back to say how happy he was for her and that he and Neil had also made some new friends so they were finding their way around in a group which made life a lot easier.

Lauren was up bright and early the following morning, she wanted to explore the campus a little and find out where her first lecture room was. When she was happy she knew- where she was going she went back to her room to meet Joanne because they had arranged to go to breakfast together. The girls quickly ate breakfast and headed off in different directions to begin this years' study. Lauren was soon immersed in her studies and the first year flew by, it was almost time for the summer break. She had invited Joanne to stay with her and her parents for the holiday because Joanne's parents were both away from their homes. Her father was away on business and her mother was on another exotic holiday with her live in lover. Joanne happily accepted the invitation because she didn't fancy staying in Oxford on her own.

When they arrived at Lauren's house her mother was watching through the front window for them. At first sight of them she raced to the front door to open it. She gave both girls a hug as they entered the house, she felt elated to have her daughter home again, even if it was only for a few short weeks. Claire closed the door behind them and ushered them into the kitchen where her husband was waiting. He hugged his daughter tightly and placed a gentle kiss on the top of her head.

"It's wonderful to have you both here,," he said as he placed a reassuring arm around Joanne's shoulders. Claire beckoned them all to sit around the table she placed the coffee pot in the centre and told them to help themselves. They were all too deep in conversation to hear the gentle tap on the front door before it opened and Samuel walked in. He quickly followed the sounds of talking and laughter to the kitchen where he walked in and said.

"Hello everyone, remember me?"

Claire swung round, jumped out of her chair and flung her arms around him, "Samuel," she shrieked. "You are home!"

He laughed and waltzed around the kitchen with her in his arms and said. "You missed me then?"

"Of course I missed you," she replied.

"Put me down there is someone I would like you to meet."

He quickly obliged, got a cup out of the cupboard and sat down at the table with them.

"Samuel" she said. "I would like you to meet my very good friend Joanne." "I don't know how I would have managed this last year without her."

Samuel smiled at the rather shy looking girl at the other side of the table and said, "I am pleased to meet you. any friend of Lauren's is a friend of mine."

The time flew by as the three young people all recounted the past year that they had had.

"I don't know about you three young people but mother and I are getting hungry so I think that it is time I treated us to our evening meal."

"Would you like to invite your mother and father to join us?" he asked Samuel.

"It will be nice for us all to get together for a change."

"We haven't seen much of your parents since your father retired." Richard told him.

Samuel told him that his parents had been spending a lot of time in Essex because his grand-mother had died and they had needed to sort out her estate.

"We are very sorry to hear that." Claire and Richard said in unison. "We know how much she meant to you all."

"Well, on that sad note," said Samuel. "I will take my leave of you and go and invite my parents out for that meal."

He gave Claire and Lauren a peck on the cheek and said that he would see them all in about half an hour with his parents.

An hour later and they were all settled around one long table at the back of the restaurant drinking a toast to the continued success of their children. Claire leaned over to Marion and invited her round to her house for a coffee in the morning when they would be able to catch up on what had been happening. She told Marion that she had missed her being around and she was so sorry to hear about her mother. Marion said she would love to go round for coffee, but tonight they would concentrate on their children and how wonderful it was to have them at home even for just a few short weeks. The evening went well and when eventually Claire, Richard and the two girls got home, Joanne whispered to Lauren that she thought that she was very lucky because it was as if she had two families not just one. Lauren smiled and said that it had been that way all of her life and she really did know how lucky she was.

The following morning the two women sat in Claire's kitchen deep in conversation. Marion looked at Claire and said that she had often thought about the day that they had met in the church yard. She told her how much she had appreciated the courage that she had given to her that day and also how much her friendship had meant to her over the years.

"I always felt that it was divine intervention, meeting someone who was suffering in the same way as me." She said as she leant over and gently clasped Claire's hand.

"I know." "I always felt that I gained a younger sister that day," said Claire with an obvious affection sounding in her voice.

"Now, tell me." "What happened with your mother and why on earth didn't you let me know?" "I might have been able to help in some way even if it was to just give you moral support," she said sympathetically to her young friend.

"I didn't have time to let anyone know," Marion replied. "We had a telephone call from her neighbour to say that she had fallen in the street and that she had been rushed to hospital."

"So of course we packed an overnight bag and went straight to the hospital where the Consultant told us that she had broken her right hip and ankle."

"He also told us that he couldn't operate on her until he had controlled the chest infection which mother was suffering with."

"We were with her almost constantly for the first week but they couldn't stop the infection turning to pneumonia." "She only lasted for another three days," said Marion as she broke down in tears.

"The only thing that makes me feel better about it is that we were with her at the end, she didn't die alone."

"Fortunately, with us already being there we could make all of the funeral arrangements and then we put all of mother's financial affairs and her estate into the hands of her solicitors."

Claire put her arm around her friends shoulder to try and comfort her a little. Marion leant her head on Claire and was glad to feel the warm loving care flowing freely from her friend. Her husband David had been her rock but it was only now that she felt she could release all the emotion which had been building inside of her. Marion thought to herself that Claire would never know how much she had meant to her and how grateful she was for such a dear friend.

Marion eventually lifted her head from Claire's shoulder and told her that she had let Samuel know about his grand-mother but she had suggested that he would be better not attending the funeral service. She told him that his grand-mother wouldn't want him disrupting his studies for her. She was so proud of her handsome grand-son I think that her friends were quite bored with her repeatedly telling them that he was studying to become a Veterinary Surgeon. She suddenly had a smile on her face as she remembered the way her mother had proudly spoken about her son and she couldn't hide her own pride as she recalled her happy memories.

"While I am talking about mother has just reminded me that I must give him his grand-father's gold hunter pocket watch."

"I was looking through mother's drawers to find some clean clothes for her to change into while she was in hospital when I came across it wrapped up in a box with Samuel's name on it."

"It's almost as if she knew somehow that she wouldn't be able to give it to him herself," she recalled with more than a hint of sadness in her voice.

Claire got up from the table and moved towards the kettle. "I think that it is time that we had a fresh cup of coffee."

"I will go and see where the men are and then we can all have a drink together."

"What a good idea," said Marion. "I will go and powder my nose before they come in."

Claire found the two men relaxing in her summer house reading their news papers. "I wish I had got my camera with me," she joked as she told them that there was a fresh cup of coffee in the kitchen for them.

Both men folded their papers and duly followed her into the kitchen. "Have you girls had a nice catch up?" Richard enquired with a twinkle in his eye.

"Yes. thank you," said Claire "But I bet that we haven't put the world to rights like you two," she said laughing at Richard.

"I know what you men are like when you get together." "Let's take our coffees into the lounge where we can be more comfortable," suggested Claire.

They settled in the lounge and David said, "I wonder where the children have gone today?" "They seemed to go out very early this morning."

"I have a feeling that they have gone to show Joanne some of the sights of London." His wife replied.

"I seem to remember hearing them mention taking Joanne on the London Eye and then on to the Tate Gallery". "I hope that she isn't afraid of heights," Claire said lightly.

"They all seem to be getting on very well together I notice," said Marion.

"There does appear to be a touch of chemistry on both sides," replied Claire, while silently concerning herself about her own daughters' feelings for Samuel. She tried her best but she couldn't stop feeling that those two young people belonged together. They were a match made in Heaven.

Chapter 25

Only one day left of the holidays and the girls had gone shopping by themselves for a change. They had left Samuel at home to finish an important assignment which had to be handed in when he got back to College. Unfortunately for him, try as he might he couldn't concentrate on the job in hand. He needed someone to talk to. He didn't want to trouble his parents because they were still mourning the loss of his Grandmother. His obvious choice he decided was to go and see Lauren's Mother. He had always been able to speak to her about anything and everything; she had always been a second Mother to him.

He carefully put his assignment away into his brief case and made his way along the road to Claire and Richard's house. When he arrived he tapped on the door and walked in as usual, calling Claire's name as he made his way along the hallway towards the kitchen. Claire came rushing through the back door from the garden when she heard him calling her name. Samuel was standing with his back to the kitchen sink when she entered the room. She studied him for a moment or two and noticed that he was quite obviously not his usual happy go lucky self.

"Come and sit down in the lounge with me and tell me what on earth, is wrong."

"I have never seen you looking so glum." She told him.

Samuel sat on the sofa and Claire sat in her favourite chair opposite him. She told him to take his time she was in no hurry and he could begin when he was ready. Samuel took a deep breath and said that there was something he wanted to talk to her about and that it would probably sound rather stupid to her. Claire explained to him that it didn't matter how silly it sounded she was there to help him if she could. Samuel settled back into the sofa and tried to explain that, ever since he met Joanne something peculiar had begun happening. He explained that the very first time that they met she reminded him of someone but he had no idea who. He tried to explain that there was just something about her. He told her that it was the way Joanne acted, the colour of her hair and her smile. That lovely smile which lit up her whole face she looked like an angel that he had forgotten. He looked at Claire with the look of a lost little puppy dog and she took his hand in hers as he continued by telling her of the dreams which he had started to have about a young woman named Annie.

The name struck at Claire's heart strings as she remembered her dear friend whom she only truly thought of on Michael Paul's Birthday. That day she would take a single long stemmed rose and place it on his grave in her memory. Samuel continued his story unaware of the memories which had flooded back to the woman sat in front of him. He said that the woman he had been dreaming about looked so much like Joanne with her jet black hair falling about her shoulders and those deep blue piercing eyes. But he knew that it wasn't her and he felt as though it was he himself caught up in his own dream although he thought that it couldn't possibly be him. He could even describe the old fashioned army uniform which the man in his dream wore and the silken gowns that the young woman wore. He looked at her intently and told her that it was as if Joanne had unlocked distant memories but he didn't understand of what, or of whom.

Claire listened intently to everything that Samuel was saying and the more he told her the more she thought about Annie. She was dumbfounded. How could he possibly know anything about a woman who had died before he was born? She told him to excuse her for a moment while she fetched something from the other room. A few moments later Claire returned with a photograph clutched in her hand. She told Samuel that she would like him to take a look at the old lady at the centre of the photograph. She explained that the lady was her friend Annie and she wondered whether she could be the young woman in his dreams. He studied the image in front him carefully and looked at Claire with an even more confused expression than before.

"I just don't understand any of this," he said feeling even more confused than before because he was sure that the old woman in the photograph was the same person he saw in his dreams.

"Don't worry about it now," she advised him with her usual soothing manner.

"I can't explain it to you at all perhaps your subconscious mind is playing tricks on you."

"I think that the best thing you can do is accept your dreams for what they are and just get on with living your life to the full."

"I am sure that if there is any significance in your dreams it will eventually become apparent," she assured him.

Samuel kissed her on the cheek and thanked her for listening to him. He said that he felt much better for having spoken about it and he would try to put his worries to the back of his mind. He made his way to the front door with a smile on his face instead of the frown he had arrived with. Before he left he asked Claire to tell the girls that he would be at home if they wanted to go to his house. She assured him that she would and then he closed the door behind him and was gone.

Claire looked at the photograph in her hand and she thought about the day that it had been taken. Richard had taken it the day that they first went to see Annie in her new flat. She was like a child with a new toy as she gave them a guided tour of her home. It was such a pity that she didn't live long enough to really enjoy it Claire thought to herself as she carefully placed the photograph back into the album she had taken it from. Samuel's conversation with her had brought many memories flooding back to her mind and she found herself thinking about Wendy. She hadn't heard from her for about six months now and that was most unusual.

While the children had been growing up Wendy had been a regular visitor to their home. In fact Claire had often joked about being able to tell the time by her visits, always 2 o'clock on the dot. She remembered the look on Wendy's face when she and Richard had asked her to be Lauren's God Mother she couldn't have been more proud and had accepted the invitation immediately. Whenever she visited when Lauren was growing up she always had a surprise hidden on her person somewhere. Lauren had great fun trying to pick which pocket her surprise was hidden in. As Claire recalled Lauren was about 8 years old when Wendy announced that she was going to take early retirement. She had seen an old French farmhouse for sale in a magazine and she was thinking of buying it and turning it into a bed and breakfast holiday home. It all seems so long ago now Claire thought to herself as she remembered the day that they said, "Goodbye and good luck," to her as she began her journey to France and her new life. The farmhouse stood overlooking a lush valley filled with grape vines and surrounded by olive trees. On a sunny day the view took her breath away with the sun dancing on the ripening grapes and the leaves blowing playfully in the warm breeze.

It had taken Wendy twelve months of hard work, working alongside local tradesmen to transform the outbuildings of the farmhouse into the modern holiday accommodation which she now possessed. Claire and her family and of course their friends had a holiday there at least once a year while Lauren and Samuel were growing up. The children loved the freedom they had to go exploring on their own. As they grew older they was allowed to go dowm into the valley where the grape harvesters were working and it didn't take them long to learn enough French words so that they could communicate with the locals. In the evenings the two of them loved to sit on the porch (which Wendy had designed and had built onto the front of the house) and watch the sun go down in the distant horizon. This, they thought, was the most perfect place on earth and they were always sad when they had to leave it behind and go back home to the real world. Lauren silently promised herself that one day she would own a place like that and when she did she would never leave it. Claire smiled as she recalled watching her daughter day dreaming while she sat on the top step leading to the porch in front of that now pretty farmhouse. Tubs and hanging baskets were filled to overflowing with brightly coloured scented flowers at the front of the house. Claire had wished Wendy every success with the business and had told her how much they were all missing her visits at home. The two women hugged each other and they both instinctively knew- that their friendship would always survive the distance between them.

She didn't know how long she had been lost in her own little world reminiscing about the past but it wasn't long before her peace was shattered when the girls arrived back home with their hands full of shopping bags. "It looks as if you two have had a good day," she said as she remarked on the number of bags which the girls' had dropped onto the coffee table as they slumped into the sofa and kicked their shoes off. The girls only laughed with her and quickly began showing her what they had bought. Joanne got a small gift bag from the bottom of one of the shopping bags and gave it to Claire. She told her that it was just a small gift to say thank you for letting her stay and for making her feel like one of the family. Claire opened it to find a small box lying at the bottom. She took the box out of the bag and opened it to reveal a small Chrystal Friendship Angel. She was delighted but told Joanne she was a silly girl for buying it although she knew that she would treasure such a kind gift.

When the girls had rested and had a cup of coffee she told them that Samuel was waiting at home for them. They thanked her and then disappeared up the road towards Samuel's house. Richard had finished his chores in the garden for the day so he came into the house, put his slippers on and settled down for a peaceful afternoon. He had heard the girls go out again so he knew that he wouldn't be disturbed. Claire joined her husband on the sofa and snuggled up to him, she put her head on his shoulder and they both enjoyed a quiet time together before the inevitable chatter that came when the three young ones got together.

A short while later Lauren came home on her own she told her parents that Samuel and Joanne were going to the pictures. They had asked her to go with them but she didn't want to be a gooseberry so she had declined. Her parents gave each other a knowing look because they both had always thought that Samuel and Claire belonged together but as time went on it seemed less and less likely that they would ever get together in a loving relationship.

The clock struck eleven as Claire, Richard and the two girls sat around the kitchen table. Claire couldn't help but notice the glow in Joanne's face and the twinkle in her eyes. It was obvious to her that Samuel and Joanne were, now an item and while she told her that she was very happy for her she couldn't help but wonder how Lauren would handle it in the future. She put her thoughts on the subject to the back of her mind because this was their last night to be together like this for the foreseeable future. Tomorrow the three young people would be back to College and University to continue their studies and she was going to miss them all.

Chapter 26

They all quickly settled back into the routine of studying and their days seemed to fly by. Lauren became so engrossed in her studies that she didn't realise that her contact with Samuel had dwindled to almost nothing while her friend had been talking or texting him constantly for the past six months. Of course she was happy for them both but she couldn't shake the gnawing ache she had in the pit of her stomach whenever she heard them talking to one another. She tried to tell herself that she was being stupid and that there were plenty of young men asking her out and it was. now time for her to move on with her life. She had a wide circle of friends now and she made a conscious decision to spend more time with them and less with Joanne. She felt that she needed to give her two special friends the space they needed to allow their relationship to flourish without worrying about her. She could always comfort herself with the knowledge that Joanne was in her final year and would be leaving in a few short months. She was thinking of this as she hurried around the corner of the building, heading towards her next lecture room when she ran headlong into a man she thought was another student and sent his books flying in every direction. She stood rooted to the spot with embarrassment, how could she have been so clumsy? Why, wasn't she looking where she was going? She could only stand and apologise while she watched him pick up his books and then chase across the grass trying desperately to catch his papers which were being blown in every- direction. Finally, he had retrieved all his belongings and was holding them safely under his arm. She tried to apologise again but he could only stand laughing at her. She began to feel quite angry' with him and asked him what he thought he was laughing at.

"Do excuse me," he said and then told her that he was imagining how silly he must have looked chasing in all 26 directions after a few pieces of paper blowing in the wind. She looked at him and started to laugh herself as she had to agree that he had looked quite comical. He stretched out his hand to shake hers and introduced himself as Ian Duncan.

"Hello Ian Duncan, I am Lauren Pearson and I am very pleased to meet you," she said with a hint of a smile on her lips.

"It would appear that we are both going to be late for our lectures this morning," he observed taking a quick glance at his watch.

"Would you meet me for coffee at lunch time?" he asked timidly.

"There is a nice coffee shop just down the road which I like to use whenever I am in Oxford." he told her.

"I would like to," she replied laughing again as she noticed a smudge of wet grass on the side of his face. She pointed it out to him and he immediately wiped it off with his hand.

Lauren arrived at her lecture looking rather flushed having run the rest of the way to the lecture room. She apologised to the lecturer and the rest of the class for her late arrival and tried to listen to what the lecturer was saying but her mind kept wandering back to the early morning event. Unfortunately her absent mindedness didn't go un-noticed by the lecturer Professor Deveraux, because as class was dismissed he said that he hoped that Miss Pearson would be more attentive next time that they met. She assured him that she would and apologised again for her tardiness.

She arrived at the coffee shop more or less at the same time as Ian and he showed her to his favourite table in a small alcove at the back of the shop. He explained that he liked to sit there because it was out of the way of the draught whenever the door was opened. He smiled at her and whisperd, "Method in my madness," and she smiled back at him in agreement. They ordered a large latte each and chatted as if they were old friends, they were both surprised at how comfortable they felt in each others' company. They soon discovered that they both had a free afternoon and they decided to catch a bus and go into Oxford town. The strong wind which had been blowing in the morning had lightened considerably so when they got into town they went for a leisurely stroll along the river bank.

As they walked side by side along the pathway at the side of the river their hands accidentally touched for a brief moment and in that instant she knew that here was someone special. She couldn't believe the warm tingling sensation which was in danger of engulfing her whole body. He reached out and took her hand in his as they walked and it felt like the most natural thing in the world. As they continued walking he told her that he had been invited to speak to the Egyptology students that morning. He explained that he was in England on leave from his job as a Curator at the museum in Cairo. He specialised in

Sanskrit Translation and when his friend Professor Lewis, head of the Egyptology department heard that he was in England he invited him to speak to his students. Lauren was fascinated by what he had to say and clung on to ever) word as he described his feelings as he descended into the old tombs of the kings. He described in graphic detail some of the wonderful wall paintings he had been privileged to see. She had so many questions to ask him but he told her that that was enough about him. He wanted to know something about the beautiful girl at his side. She blushed and smiled and said that compared to his life hers was very boring.

She told him a little about home and her parents and of course Samuel and his family. He looked at her with a hint of a frown and asked if he needed to be worried about Samuel. She laughed and told him that Samuel was now very much involved with her friend Joanne. He looked relieved, gave her a cheeky smile and said that he was pleased to hear that.

Lauren looked at her watch, it was nearly 5 o'clock. "I shall have to get back soon," she said.

"I have arranged to meet some friends at The Kings Head for a drink at 7 o'clock you are welcome to come too if you like," she told him.

He declined her kind offer because he felt that it would be more prudent not to mix with the students too much socially. It was only then that she realised the age and social standing difference between them. He was a mature man in a responsible position who travelled the world and her friends were all young people just starting out in life. They made their way back to the University grounds where he said he would leave her. As they said, "Goodbye" she looked into his kind tanned face and his soft blue green eyes and thought how much younger he looked than his thirty five years. He thanked her for a very pleasant afternoon and asked if he could see her again before he left for Cairo at the end of the week. She said that she would love to and they arranged to meet on Wednesday before he flew home on Friday. They shook hands and went their separate ways.

Lauren went back to her room feeling as if she was floating on a cloud. What was she thinking of? She had only just met him but she felt as though she had known him all her life. That evening flew by in a blur of excitement her mind kept wandering back to the wonderful afternoon she had spent by the riverside and the handsome man she had spent it with.

Chapter 27

Claire was happily humming along to her favourite tune when she was disturbed by the telephone ringing. It was Marion at the other end and she sounded in a terrible panic as she begged Claire to come to her house and bring Richard with her. David had been taken ill during the night and he had been taken into hospital. Through Marion's sobbing and tears Claire was able to make out that David had suffered a stroke. Fortunately, they were able to tell her before she went home that morning that her husband appeared to have had a mini stroke. They assured her that it was possible for him to make an almost full recovery from it. Claire listened intently and then told her friend to put the phone down, put the kettle on and she and Richard would be with her in a few moments.

Ten minutes later and the three friends were discussing David's condition over a cup of coffee. Claire placed a comforting arm around her friend and told her that if she wanted her to she would go with her to visit David later that day. Marion was only too pleased to accept her friend's offer to accompany her to the hospital. They then sat in silence as they finished their coffee, each deep in their own thoughts of David and none of them inclined to make trivial conversation. Claire did wonder whether or not they should contact Samuel to tell him about his father's condition but Marion said, "No". She didn't want to worry her son at this time, he had enough to think about with his studies and besides which there was nothing that he could do she assured Claire. She also pointed out that it would be different if David's condition had been life threatening, thank goodness it wasn't. Claire agreed with her friends' thinking that it wasn't fair to worry the children unnecessarily. Her two friends suggested that Marion get some sleep as she looked totally drained.

"I do have another headache," Marion confessed. "Worrying about David has triggered it off again," she admitted as she held her throbbing head in her hands.

"I will go and get some pain killers and then have a lie down and hope that the pain will be gone when I awake," she told her friends.

They waited until she was settled before leaving her to get some sleep. They quietly closed the door behind them, locked it and then made their way home. On the way Richard turned to his wife and told her that he was becoming more and more concerned about the number of headaches and dizzy spells which Marion had been suffering from lately. He asked Claire to speak to Marion and try to get her to see her GP about them. He confessed that he thought it would be advisable sooner rather than later to which his wife agreed. While she agreed with her husband she thought it better to approach the subject at a later date when David was back at home and well on the mend. He agreed that she was probably right and the subject was dropped for the time being. Mid afternoon and the two friends called to collect Marion and take her to the hospital to see her husband.

"Have you got everything he needs in here?" Claire enquired as she lifted the overnight bag which Marion had packed for her husband.

"I hope so," Marion replied as she swallowed two more pain killers.

"Your sleep hasn't done your headache much good then?" observed Richard.

Marion agreed but said that it would probably be better the next day after she had had a good nights' sleep.

Richard nodded in agreement and gently patted her hand with his. Marion looked at her two best friends and thought how lucky she was to have them they were always there for her ready and willing to help with any situation. They had been friends now for over twenty years and she had been thankful for every day that passed. A week later and David w-as at home recovering well. His speech was almost normal although he had to consider what he was going to say for a little longer than normal. While he was able to walk short distances and use his hands a little it was going to take quite a lot of physiotherapy to build his strength up again. That didn't cause him too much concern though because he was just happy to be at home again with the people he loved. He told his wife that he was glad that she hadn't told Samuel about his illness because he wouldn't have wanted to disturb his son's studies, not when he was doing so well. His pride for his son couldn't have been more obvious.

Over the coming weeks David's health improved beyond everyone's expectations and he had even started to do little jobs around the house. He couldn't help but notice that his darling wife seemed to be in constant pain and she was beginning to look very tired and drawn. Her usual glowing pink cheeks were now constantly pale, almost ashen looking. Her eyes surrounded by dark circles had lost their sparkle and appeared quite sunken in her face. He had quietly become very concerned about her and decided that today he wouldn't accept her dismissal of his fears. She was busying herself in the kitchen as usual but David called her to come and sit with him. He had something important he wanted to discuss with her. A few moments later she sat at his side and he gently held her hand in his as he told her that he wanted her to go and see their GP. He told her that he had been aware for a long time that things weren't right with her and he didn't want her to leave it any longer before she got some sort of help. He said that he couldn't stand by and watch her suffer any longer. He knew that she had put her own health to one side while she looked after him and he was very grateful to her for what she had done for him. But now, he told her was time for her to think of herself. She lay her head on his chest and let her tears flow, how relieved she felt as she realised that she didn't have to try to hide her condition from David any more. She promised that she would make the appointment as soon as possible. She told him that she hadn't wanted to worry him and that he had been her priority.

He kissed her tenderly and said that he understood but he would be more worried if she didn't go and get some sort of help. Two days later Marion sat in the Doctors' Surgery with Claire at her side. He looked across his desk at her and asked her to describe her symptoms in as much detail as she could. He nodded, got out of his chair and examined her eyes and ears and told her that he wanted her to go to the hospital for a scan. He wrote a letter of contact to the Consultant as she sat there. He told her that he couldn't be sure of what was causing the problem and that was why he wanted her to get the scan as soon as possible.

The following week Marion sat nervously in the hospital waiting room for her name to be called. How grateful she was that her friend sat by her side trying to make light conversation to take her mind off the scan. Outwardly she was trying to put on a brave face but inwardly she felt terrified. In her own mind she already had an idea of what her problem was and she thought that today she was just going to get the confirmation which she was dreading. She looked at the clock on the wall it read ten o'clock, her appointment time. Just then she heard her name being called. She rose slowly from out of her seat and Claire asked her if she wanted her to go with her but she refused her kind offer. Just knowing that she was there waiting for her was enough she said smiling at her friend. She suggested that Claire go the cafeteria and have a cup of coffee while she waited because she could be about an hour she informed her. Claire wished her well and said that she would get a coffee and that she would be waiting there when Marion was finished.

An hour later the two friends were walking towards the Consultants room. Claire rested a comforting hand on her friends arm because she could see the fear in her friends face. They didn't have to wait many minutes after they reached the Consultants' waiting room before a nurse called them in. When they entered his room he looked up from the scan pictures which he was studying carefully. He beckoned them to take a seat in front of his desk and then continued with his scrutiny of the pictures in front of him. When he had finished he looked at Marion and introduced himself as Mr Ahmed. He asked whether her husband had come with her because he felt that what he had to say would be better said with her husband present. She told him that he was recovering from a stroke and she didn't want to worry him unnecessarily. He nodded his head and said that he could understand what she meant. She told him that her friend Claire was as close as any family member and she was there to give her the support she needed. He leaned back in his chair slightly and looking Marion straight in the eyes he said that what he had to tell her might come as a bit of a shock. She looked him in the eye and told him she wanted to know the truth about her condition. She said that she had already got an idea of what he was going to say and she wanted straight facts from him.

He told her that the headaches which she had been having were being caused by a tumour about the size of an egg situated at the base of the scull. He also said that from what he could see from the scan it was enclosing blood vessels to the brain and he felt that it would be too dangerous to operate at this time. She sat in stunned silence for what seemed an eternity although it was only a few moments. She admitted that she had been thinking in her own mind that it could have been a tumour but hearing someone else confirm her thoughts was devastating. He told her to sit and gather her thoughts for a moment while he left the room to speak to a colleague who was more familiar with this particular tumour.

When he had left the room Marion broke down in tears, she clung on to Claire as if trying to cling on to life itself. Claire placed a hand on Marion's head as she leant on her shoulder and Claire couldn't stop herself shedding tears for her friend and the situation she found herself in. Where would she find the strength from to cope with looking after David and face the dismal looking future which lay ahead of her?

Ten minutes later he introduced the two women to his colleague Mr Jamieson who he explained was a specialist in this field. Mr Ahmed then made his apologies and left the room to tend to another patient. Mr Jamieson tried to reassure Marion that they would do everything possible to help her. He explained that what Mr Ahmed had told her was quite right the tumour could not be operated on in its present state. However, he assured her that there was treatment that they could give her which should reduce the size of the tumour and then they could look at their options again. He explained the course of chemotherapy which he would like her to agree to have. He told her that she would have to spend one week a month in hospital while she was receiving the chemotherapy and the course would last for six months. He also said that it was imperative for the treatment to begin as soon as possible, he would give her time to make arrangements for her husband's care and then he wanted her in hospital having her first course of treatment. He informed her that he would be contacting the Oncology Ward and they would send her appointment in the post. The two women shook his hand and thanked him for the considerate way he had dealt with the matter and Marion told him that she would wait to receive the appointment date.

The two women walked in silence towards the cafeteria, they were both in desperate need of a strong sweet coffee. After they had ordered and had taken their seats Marion looked at Claire and admitted that she was expecting that diagnosis. She said she had hoped that she was wrong but in her heart of hearts she thought that she was right. Claire also confessed that she and Richard had been thinking along the same lines but not for a moment did they think that it would be inoperable. She also told her friend that she was not to worry about David when she had to be in hospital because either David could stop with them or Richard would stay at their house with him if that was what David preferred. I am so grateful that we have you as friends Marion told her with the slightest hint of a smile at the comers of her mouth. Claire asked if she wanted her to stay while she told David but Marion declined her kind offer and said that she preferred to tell him when they were alone. With their coffee finished the two women made their way home neither wanting to speak, they both had too many thoughts racing through their heads. Claire dropped Marion off at her house and then made her way down the street to her own home where Richard would be waiting for her.

Marion entered the lounge and found David asleep in his chair. She stood and watched him for a few moments before she gently touched his hand to rouse him from his slumbers. He looked into her eyes and noticed the moisture lying within them. Slowly he rose from his chair and held his wife in his arms not wanting to let her go. He kissed her slowly and lovingly on her lips as he had done so many times over the past twenty' five years. He moved her towards the sofa where they sat side by side and he asked her what had been said at the hospital. She explained everything to him as simply as she could, she didn't want to cause him any un-necessary concern. She felt that he had enough to worry about with his own health issues. David put his arm around his wife and told her that they would get through it together. He would always be there for her, however, he said that this time they needed to tell Samuel and she agreed to tell him when he came home for the summer break in a few weeks time.

A week later Marion was sitting in a comfortable chair next to her hospital bed waiting for her first course of chemotherapy which she was dreading. Fortunately she wasn't alone. She was in a side ward with three other women who were all awaiting the same fate as herself. They each chatted easily among themselves as they endured the discomfort of the needles and the chemicals flowing into their bodies. Each one praying, that this would be a life saving treatment for them especially the young woman who sat opposite to her because she had two young children at home who needed to have their mother with them. The other two women were older and had grown up families and very similar situation to Marion herself. It was a gruelling week which all of the women were pleased to see come to an end and they were free to go home to re-cooperate for the following three weeks before beginning the second session.

Once home Marion and David busied themselves making plans for when Samuel would be home from College. They missed him so much when he was away at College it would be wonderful to have him at home for a few weeks. Although she knew he would be cross with her for not telling him about the health problems which she and his father had suffered in the past year. However, she comforted herself with the knowledge that he would scold her a little but he would soon get over it. She could hardly wait to feel her son's arms around her as he gave her his usual bear hug.

The week flew by and soon the day which both sets of parents were waiting for arrived. Samuel was the first to arrive home calling to his parents as he walked through the house. He found them sitting on the patio basking in the warm sunshine and enjoying a much needed laugh at a private joke between the two of them. He stood a short distance from his parents and studied them for a moment before he spoke. His mother jumped up out of her chair and ran to him, a smile spread all over her face. She pulled him over to where they were sitting and told him to stay there while she fetched him a cold drink. Her joy at seeing her son was overflowing and the things she had to tell him could wait until later. She and David had so many questions to ask him about his studies and how he was progressing. He told them to slow down, he was doing well and he was looking forward to having a rest and putting it behind him for a few weeks.

It was later that evening that he took his mother on one side and asked what was happening with both her and his father. He told her that he only had to look at them to know' that things were not right with either of them. Marion asked him to sit beside her and she would try and explain what had been going on. She apologised to her son for not wanting to tell him while he was studying. She informed him that it had been a joint decision between her and his father to try and protect him from any worry about them. He nodded and said that he understood that but now he was home he wanted details and she was not to spare him any of them. She agreed and told him first about his father's stroke but she assured him that his father was almost back to how he was before the stroke. She also told him that his father was no longer under the Doctor's supervision which she confessed was a huge relief for her. It was then that she looked at her son with a very serious expression and told him that now' she had to tell him about herself which she admitted was a very hard subject to approach. He listened intently as his mother explained to him about her condition and the treatment which she had just started. She explained that she had to tell him face to face not over the telephone. She also insisted that he was not to worry she had a feeling that everything was going to be alright. He told her that he couldn't believe how she had shouldered everything on her own. She should have let him know he told her almost distraught as he thought of what the outcome could have been. She placed a loving hand on the side of his face and told him that the last thing that she and his father wished was for him to worry' and at the moment they were both doing well. She insisted that they take each day as it comes with no fuss and he had his whole life in front of him and he should live his life to the full without concerning himself about them.

"Changing the subject," said Marion with a mischievous twinkle in her eye. "How are things coming along with you and Joanne, I have not heard you speak about her for a while?"

He looked at his mother and told her that he hadn't heard from her for some time. The last time that they had spoken she told him that she might have a job opportunity coming up but she couldn't give him any details as yet. She told him that she had no idea what the post was or even where it was. Julian an old school friend had contacted her and said that he had her in mind for an exciting new venture as soon as her finals were finished. He confided in his mother that she had sounded so excited about the prospect that he couldn't put a damper on things by letting his true feelings be known. He couldn't be responsible for stopping her from doing the things that she wanted. She was a free agent and he had to respect that.

Chapter 28

T he following day Lauren arrived home to find Samuel sitting talking with her parents. On the surface it appeared like old times with the four of them all together but this time Lauren felt that there was something quite different. While Samuel gave her his usual bear hug his heart didn't seem to be in it. She didn't need to ask what the problem was, she already knew that he was disappointed that Joanne hadn't come home with her and there was nothing that she could do about it. She hadn't heard from Joanne since she had left for her appointment with Julian and she could only assume that Samuel hadn't either. Her parents said that they needed to go out and they would leave the two of them to catch up while they were gone. Lauren tried to lighten the mood but without much success as she noticed his eyes begin to well up with tears.

She sat beside him as she begged him to tell her what was wrong. It was only then that he relayed everything about his parents illnesses. She was aware of the pent up anger and disbelief he felt at his parents keeping such important situations from him. They should have known that he would want to know and he should have had the opportunity to be there and to share it with them. Lauren did her best to console him and make him realise that his parents were doing what they thought was best for him. They didn't want to jeopardise his future by taking him out of College and away from his studies. She said that she sympathised with their decision and thought that they had no other choice. He reluctantly smiled and finally agreed to her way of thinking.

"I don't know what I would do without you sometimes," he admitted. He thanked her and for the first time since they met that day he gave her a hug which she could recognise as coming from the Samuel that she knew and loved.

He looked at his watch and said that he would have to get home soon his mother was getting him something special for lunch. "But before I go has Joanne said anything to you about us?" he enquired.

She had to admit that she hadn't. "In fact," she told him, Joanne had said very little about anything since Julian had been in touch with her. She seemed to be in a world of her own she told him. She did however say that as soon as she knew what was happening she would be here to discuss it with you thoroughly. She was pleased to see the smile which spread across his wonderful, handsome face which she had loved all of her life. She was happy for him but she couldn't stop that ridiculous pang of jealousy which cut her like a knife. Silently she admonished herself for being so stupid. She told herself that she had Ian in her life now but even that fact didn't ease the unexplainable pain she felt at the thought of Samuel and Joanne being together. Before he left to go back home they arranged to go for a drink that evening.

"Somewhere noisy and lively so that we can both relax and forget what is happening around us for a short time," he told her with that familiar twinkle in his eyes.

Her heart raced for a moment as she saw the old familiar Samuel re-appear before her and suddenly she realised how much she had missed him over the last twelve months. She had been so engrossed in her studies, Ian and everything else going on around her that she had pushed all thoughts of Samuel to the back of her mind. She knew that it was a self preservation mechanism which she had triggered herself, even so the thought of it made her feel rather sad and sorry for herself. She looked in the mirror, tied her long tresses up into a pony tail and told herself to stop thinking like that. He was a brother figure and no more.

She hurried into the kitchen and prepared lunch ready for when her parents got home. It had been a long time since they all sat down together for a meal as a family and she was really looking forward to the intimacy of it. She had always considered herself very fortunate to have such a close knit family life. She loved her parents dearly and she always knew that they thought the world of her. Even though they had been older parents than her contemporaries she always had an abundance of one to one time with both parents and for that she would be always grateful.

The following four weeks flew by with Samuel spending more time helping his father to do his chores in the garden which to his surprise he enjoyed more than he thought he would. He had insisted that for the most time his father sit on a garden chair and supervise. They were both taken by surprise at how well they worked together. His father had always considered the garden to be his domain but now he enjoyed sharing it with his son. Samuel also accompanied his mother when she had to go to the hospital for her next course of treatment although she insisted that he didn't visit her during the week. She didn't want him to see her at her lowest when she knew how ill she would be feeling. She did however agree to him meeting her and taking her home when the week was finished. He appreciated the fact that she wanted to involve him in her illness and he understood why, she didn't want him to become too involved.

The fifth week arrived and still the two friends hadn't heard a word from Joanne. They were both secretly becoming a little concerned about her when Samuel had a text message to say that she was at the train station and would be with them in half an hour. He quickly washed and changed and waited for her to arrive. He didn't have to wait long before the front door bell rang, he opened the door and Joanne stood in front of him looking beautiful with the bright sunlight playing on her long black hair. He scooped her up in his arms and planted a kiss firmly on her soft pink mouth. He led her through the house and out into the back garden which his father had now vacated. She sat on the swing which still hung from the apple tree and Samuel sat on the grass beside her. He had so many questions he wanted to ask but she told him that she wanted to enjoy this moment as it was and she would tell him everything later. He reluctantly agreed and fetched them both a long cold glass of juice and they spent the next hour more or less in silence as they enjoyed the closeness of each other. He rang Lauren and told her that Joanne was with him and invited her to join them later that evening.

Evening arrived and the three friends sat in Samuel's lounge. His parents were going out for a drink to the local pub with Richard and Claire so they had the house to themselves for a couple of hours. Lauren looked at Joanne and asked how she had managed to get such a wonderful tan. "You look amazing," she told her. Joanne smiled and said that it wasn't so surprising as she had just got back from Africa. Samuel and Lauren looked at her in disbelief.

"What on earth were you doing in Africa?" Samuel asked hardly knowing what to say.

"That was where I had to meet with Joshua," she told them and then she explained exactly what she had been doing and where she went to.

Joshua had taken Holy Orders and was now 'Father Joshua.' He had been placed in charge of a Missionary School in Mombasa which had been purpose built for five to ten year olds and he desperately needed a Head of Maths and English. He had remembered from years ago the Joanne had an interest in working in a school such as this, so she was the first person he thought of to ask. She said that she was amazed when she got there at how modern the school was and that it was the kind of school she wanted to work in. She felt that it had so much potential to help all of the young children in that area. In fact she told them that the school took children from as far away as a ten mile radius. The excitement in her face was unmistakeable; her eyes shone with delight as she spoke about what the future could be for her. Samuel and Lauren sat in silence as they listened to her talking, unable to hide the excitement she was feeling. Then quite suddenly she stopped. She looked at her friends for the first time since she began telling her story and realised how sad and disappointed they were looking. She had been so full of her own excitement that she hadn't thought how her news would affect the two people who sat there listening.

She turned to Samuel and asked him to please try and understand that this was something which she had to do. She told him that she knew that he had feelings for her just as she had feelings for him but this was an opportunity which might never come again and she had to grab it with both hands. She also told him that the school was only twenty miles away from a Game Reserve which could benefit from employing its own Veterinary Surgeon. She knew of his passion for big cats and thought that a position there could be ideal for both of them. He listened intently to what she was saying and told her that it was something he could think about for the future. After all he reminded her he had only completed two of the five years it would take him to qualify'.

Lauren couldn't help but feel desolated for her best friend. He had often confided in her that he had hoped for a loving relationship with Joanne and now it was obvious to her that his dreams and wishes had just been demolished. Joanne tried to persuade him that it need not be the end of their relationship. This post only meant that she would like to put it on hold for twelve months as this was the length of the contract which she had signed. Samuel said that he would need time to think about everything which she had told him. He couldn't and wouldn't make any decisions at the present time. He did however wish her well and told her that he hoped she could make all of her future dreams and wishes come true.

It was with a heavy heart that he closed the door behind the two girls as they made their way back to Lauren's house. Joanne confided in Lauren that she hadn't realised how difficult it would be to tell Samuel of her plans but it was something she felt she had to do face to face.

Lauren found it very difficult to know how to react to her friends' news. She truly wanted to be happy for her but at the same time she could feel Samuel's pain. Finally she asked Joanne when she thought she might be going back to Africa and she told her that she was booked on a plane leaving Gatwick in two days time. The following day the girls saw very' little of Samuel as he said that he had made other arrangements and he would be away for most of the day. Lauren and her mother decided to take Joanne on a shopping trip partly to try and take her mind off the effect that her news had had on Samuel and also to get the last minute things that she needed to take with her.

That evening as the girls sat chatting and discussing future plans the atmosphere was very different between them. The usual light heartedness between them had been replaced by a sadness which neither of them wanted to talk about. Lauren did eventually tell Joanne that she understood that she had to follow her dreams, her own way in life and she was sure that Samuel would come to terms with her decision. The time was getting late and before they went to bed the two girls hugged and promised that they would keep in touch whenever possible. The next morning Joanne thanked both Richard and Claire for allowing her to stay with them and for all that they had done for her. She hugged them both before she made the journey back to Oxford where she finished packing her belongings which she was taking to Africa with her. She asked Lauren to dispose of anything she found which was not of use to her and which she had left behind. Lauren promised she would do it as soon as she got back to their room. She understood that she needed to clear any of Joanne's belongings before her new room-mate arrived to begin her three years of study.

It was later that day when Lauren went to see Samuel. She wasn't sure how she would find him but she was determined to let him know that she was there for him, that she would always support him through any crisis which he might have in his life. When she arrived at his house she was very pleasantly surprised. Samuel welcomed her with his usual bear hug and told her that she need not have worried about him. He told her that he had been in contact with Joanne that morning and had found out the time of her train. He had been at the station to see her off and had given her a star burst brooch as a keepsake and as a reminder of him. He said that he had had the time he needed to think things over and had realised that Joanne must have had a calling and he didn't want to get in the way of that. They had also agreed that when her contract was finished in a years' time she would come back to England and try to find employment here. In the mean time he told Lauren he had enough to think about with his parents failing health and the prospect of another three years of study. The two friends then spent the last few days of the summer break in each others' company just as they had always done. They both agreed that it was like old times again and that they would not change anything which had happened over the past two years.

All too soon the two friends were off in opposite directions again. Each one knowing that hard study lay- before them if they were to gain the qualifications which they were both working so hard for.

Chapter 29

T he following months flew by and Samuel was overjoyed to receive a phone call from his mother one day telling him that her condition had gone into remission and that his father was doing so well that they were going to go with Claire and Richard to France. It had been some time since the friends had seen Wendy and they were all looking forward to spending some quality time together in that beautiful French country side.

It was a warm balmy evening when the friends arrived at the farmhouse and Wendy had a light meal of chicken, salad and bread prepared for them. It looked so inviting sitting on a table situated in a shady corner on the porch. Wendy welcomed them all with open arms and a smile which lit up the whole of her face. She was overjoyed to see them all and quickly beckoned them to sit and eat. She poured each of them a glass of local white sparkling wine which they raised in a toast to their friendship and wished that theirs may never be broken. When the friends had finished eating the two women told Wendy to stay where she was while they cleared the table and did the washing up. When it was done the five friends sat talking and reminiscing until late in the evening. There was so much news to catch up with and

Wendy wanted to know every thing about her two favourite young people. She was so proud of the people that they had become and she wished that she could have seen more of them but of course under the circumstances that was impossible. She gently sighed to herself and whispered "ce- la- vie."

It was David who finally said that he going to retire for the night. They had had a long day and he was sure that Marion was ready for her bed too. She nodded in agreement with her husband and they asked Wendy to kindly show them to their room. When she returned Wendy found Claire and Richard sitting at the old Scrub top table in the kitchen. The kettle was beginning to boil and three coffee cups were place nearby on the work surface. Claire smiled as she looked at Wendy and said. "I always feel as if I have come to my second home whenever I am here in this beautiful place." "I love the cosy feel of this house and the location is what dreams are made of."

She then walked over to the window to drink in the wonderful view of the vineyard which spread out across the valley before her. Slowly she turned away from the view and joined the others at the table where they drank their coffees in a contented silence. It was Wendy who finally broke the silence when she told Claire and Richard that tomorrow she wanted to take them on a tour of the vineyard and the adjoining winery because she had a proposition to put to them. But for now she suggested that it was time that they all got a good nights' sleep.

Early next morning the four friends awoke to the smell of a full English breakfast being cooked. The aroma drifted all through the farmhouse. Wendy was in the process of plating the breakfasts up when the four friends entered the kitchen. Richard turned to his wife and joked that she didn't spoil him like that when they were at home. Claire only laughed and told him that she spoiled him enough without cooking breakfast for him as well.

Breakfast over and David said that he hoped no-one would be offended but he and Marion were going to walk into the village and hire a car for the day. They wanted to do some exploring and they thought it was a good idea to give the others some quality time on their own. They all agreed and when David and Marion were gone Wendy told Claire and Richard to sit down while she explained what she had in mind. She told them that the bed and breakfast business which she started when she first arrived was no longer a viable venture. But, she explained, she had recently been approached by the owner of the vineyard with a view to her purchasing it. She said that she wanted their input after they had toured around it. She said that it felt as though fate had taken a hand in what was happening especially with their timely arrival. She said that she couldn't have organised events any better herself if she had tried. They closed the door behind them and made their way into the valley and over towards the winery' where the present owner Monsieur Gairant stood waiting for them.

He welcomed them all with a warm handshake and proceeded to show them around the winery first. They were all impressed as they watched the wine making process from beginning to end. When they had completed that part of the tour he invited them to have a taste of his now quite famous Valley Red which he hoped they would enjoy. They all agreed that it was an excellent drink with its' subtle fruity flavour and full bodied aroma. "Bon," said Monsieur Gairant, as he suggested they follow him into the fields where they could inspect the bumper crop of grapes for themselves. It was beginning to get dusk as the three friends said a weary "au revoir," to Monsieur Gairant and made their way back up the hill towards the farmhouse.

"What a fantastic business idea," said Richard as they sat together in Wendy's comfortable spacious sitting room. "I am however concerned at how you think that you are going to manage such a big venture?" He said to Wendy with deep concern etched all over his face.

"That is why I wanted you to see it for yourselves," Wendy told him with an excited twinkle in her eyes. "It will probably come as a shock to you, but I wanted to know how you would feel about coming into business with me?" "As you quite rightly say the whole idea is just too much for me to cope with but if you would consider being equal partners with me it could be a very sound investment for us all."

Richard was taken aback for a moment or two. He hadn't been expecting an offer like that and it was something which he had never considered. He asked her to give him time to talk the idea over with Claire because it would be such a life changing decision for them both. She told him that she didn't expect an answer from him now and she certainly wouldn't expect a decision without Claire being involved in it. She told him to think it over and give her an answer in a couple of days when they had had a chance to think about it thoroughly. She also told him that she knew he would have to talk things through with Lauren as well. He thanked her for her kind offer and said that he would let her know in a couple of days. In the mean time they were all going to enjoy this holiday together after ail that was why they were here in the first place.

The following day the five friends made their way into Paris for the day. It was a two hour journey from the farmhouse travelling by taxi to the metro and then travelling on the train into Paris. They all had a memorable day which included drinking coffee at a pavement cafe, walking along the Champs Elyse and finally seeing Paris from the top of the Eiffel Tower. The journey back to the farmhouse was filled with happy chattering and laughter as they recalled the day which they had just spent together and they all decided that it was a day to remember and one which they would probably never experience again.

It was a very tired group of people which climbed the stairs to bed that night to make their way to a comfortable bed and a good nights' sleep. Richard suggested that he and Claire ring Lauren the next day as it was Saturday and she would have plenty of time to talk to them about Wendy's offer. Claire agreed as Richard held her tightly in his arms and she snuggled her head onto his chest. He gently kissed the top of her head before they both fell into a deep restful sleep. Next morning they woke up bright and early, the sun shining through the bedroom window and the sound of birdsong all around them. Claire looked at Richard and said. "This feels like a good day for a life changing decision." Her husband agreed as he lifted the phone to speak to their daughter.

Lauren was delighted and surprised to hear the sound of her fathers' voice on the telephone. However her first thought was what's wrong? Her father soon put her mind at rest and told her that he had something very important to discuss with her if she had the time to listen to him. She told him that she had as long as he wanted and she was eager to hear what he had to say. He explained that he and her mother were thinking of going into partnership with Wendy if she bought the vineyard, so of course it would mean them selling their home and moving to France. She told him that if that was what he and her mother wanted she was definitely in favour of the venture. She said that she was very pleased for them. She also told her father that she had some exciting news of her own. She explained that when her finals were finished she was going to South America with Ian. He had been invited to a new dig which was due to start in August and he had asked her to go with him. He was resigning from his post at the museum so that he could concentrate on his first passion which was of course archaeology. In the mean time she promised him that she and Ian would arrange to spend some time with them during the summer so that they could discuss everything in finer detail. With the call ended he replaced the receiver and gave his wife the thumbs up. Lauren sounded really excited for us he told his wife and she said that if it is what we want we should go ahead with it. He grabbed his wife around the waist and swung her around then he put her feet firmly back on the ground, kissed her tenderly on the lips and said, "This is where we start an exciting new chapter in our lives and I can't wait."

An hour later and the two of them sat down with Wendy and told her that they would be very happy to join her in this new venture. They would of course need to sell their property in England so that they would have their share of the deposit on the vineyard. It was then that Wendy gave them a huge shock. She informed them both that she didn't want any monetary help from them because she had already decided to will her estate to them in the event of her death. So as she explained she didn't want any money from them for something which would eventually become theirs anyway. They were both too shocked to comprehend what was being said to them for a few moments. Wendy said that she would leave them to get over the shock while she went to see Monsieur Gairant to inform him of their decision and then they could arrange to visit a Solicitor to finalise details of the sale before travelling back home to make their arrangements there.

Claire told her husband that she was very excited at the prospect of coming to live in France but she didn't know how they were going to tell David and Marion. They had been friends and close neighbours for so many years she was afraid that they would be devastated by the news. Richard told her not to worry they would face that problem when they got home, so for now they could enjoy the time which they had left of their holiday together.

Chapter 30

One week later saw Claire and Richard walking up the road towards David and Marion's house. Both were nervous of how- they were going to tell their friends of their plans for the future but they agreed that it was something which needed doing sooner rather than later. When they arrived David invited them to sit in the garden.

"It would be a pity not to take advantage of such glorious weather," he told them as he gestured to them to sit.

Richard said that he was finding it difficult to know where to begin but he and his wife had some news to share with them. He, told them that it was both wonderful and at the same time sad because their lives were about to change completely. He explained about the opportunity which Wendy had put before them and that they were going to grasp it with both hands. David and Marion were stunned to hear what their friends were telling them but they agreed that it was an opportunity not to be missed. They could only wish their friends all the very best for the future and said that they wished that they were going with them.

When Claire and Richard had gone home Marion confided in her husband that she didn't know how she was going to face the future without Claire and Richard being close at hand. They had been such a tower of strength during their illnesses over the past year and she was sure that she would never meet friends like them again. Her husband took her in his arms and tried to re-assure her that they were strong enough to cope on their own if they had to although, he was getting the beginnings of an idea which he wanted to put to Richard when next he saw him.

The following weeks seemed to fly by in a haze as Claire and Richard made their preparations. The house went up for sale and was sold within a month They had both made the decision to sell it fully furnished as they didn't want the hassle of selling everything separately. It was bought by a young couple who were just married and were overjoyed at moving into a fully furnished home.

The night before they were due to leave for France the four friends met up in their favourite Italian restaurant for a goodbye meal. With their glasses filled the four friends toasted one another and David wished them "Bon Voyage." Half way through the meal David turned to Richard and told him of the idea which he and Marion had been discussing. He told him that neither of them wanted to stay where they were now that they didn't have any ties as such. The children were both grown, Lauren was now qualified and Samuel still had another two years at College and he could quite easily spend his vacations in France with them if he wished. He also said that Samuel was about to leave for Africa to meet with Joanne because she had told him that she wasn't able to come back to England. He needed to see her for himself so that he could find out what was happening with her. Lauren was already working in South America alongside Ian with another dig planned in Egypt for later in the year.

He took a deep breath and told Richard that if at all possible they would like to sell up and move to France with them. Richard was a little taken aback at what David was saying as he had no idea that they had been contemplating a move as well. Claire was overjoyed at the prospect of their friends living alongside them in France and she admitted that the thought of leaving them behind had been very hard to live with. Richard promised to discuss the possibility with Wendy as soon as they were settled into their new way of life. The following morning Claire wandered around the house for the last time, running her fingers lovingly over the furniture which had served them so well for so many love filled years. She checked that all of the drawers and wardrobes were empty of their personal belongings before packing the last bags into the boot of the car. She locked the door behind her with a heavy heart as she thought of all the wonderful memories that house held for them. With all the possessions that they wanted to take with them safely locked in the car Claire took hold of her husbands' hand. He gently squeezed her hand in his and tried to reassure her that they were doing the right thing for them and that had he still been with them, Michael Paul would have agreed whole heartedly. She knew that her husband was right but she still needed to have a few last moments at his grave to ask him to forgive her for leaving him. She had visited his grave for over a quarter of a century now and the thought of not going any more suddenly became quite unbearable. Richard knew what his wife was feeling because deep inside he felt it too and he put his arm around her waist to support her as they took the short walk to the cemetery.

They stood side by side at the foot of his small grave with tears running down both of their faces as they said a last farewell to their beloved son. They told him that their love for him would never fade even though it would not be possible to visit his resting place again. The worst feeling of all was the feeling of guilt which haunted both of them deep within their hearts. Claire clung onto her husband and sobbed. She said that she hadn't realised quite how difficult this moment would be. Then to their amazement a beam of light shone onto the cherub headstone and within that light they saw a vision of their son's face. He was smiling at them and they both heard a whispered voice telling them that everything was alright. He was happy for them and they were not to worry about leaving him, he could be with them where ever they were. The heaviness which they both had been feeling dropped away in that instant and was replaced by a feeling of euphoria. Now they had no misgivings about their future plans as they turned away from Michael Paul's grave and took their first steps towards an exciting new beginning for them both.

The first few months were very difficult for them as they had so much to learn about grape growing and the process of wine making. The hours were long from early morning to late into the evening but they loved every minute of it. It was during this time that the three friends realised where a niche could be found for David and Marion. They spent so much of their day looking after the business that there was very little time for the household chores. They were very often too tired to cook an evening meal for themselves it was just too much trouble. That was when they decided that they needed a housekeeper and Marion was exactly the person they needed especially now that Christmas was so close. Wendy suggested that they invite Marion and David to stay with them for the Christmas Holiday and then they could discuss the proposition face to face. Richard and Claire were delighted at the suggestion and couldn't wait to invite their friends to stay with them.

At home David and Marion were beginning to feel that Richard had forgotten his promise to them, Weeks had past and they hadn't heard from them at all. It was a delighted David who answered the telephone a few days later and heard Richard's voice at the other end. Richard apologised for having taken so long to ring them but as they could probably imagine life had become very hectic for them. He explained that they had realised how much they needed a housekeeper and a handy man and he and Marion would be ideal. David was thrilled at the news and said that he couldn't wait to pass on the news to his wife. Then Richard invited them both to stay with them for the Christmas holiday when they could finalise all of the details. David was a very happy man as he went to find his wife to give her the good news which he hoped would lift her spirits and make her smile again. Because she had been looking under the weather lately and he was beginning to feel quite worried about her. The smile on her face when he passed on the news made his heart sing, her joy was worth more to him than any amount of money.

Three days before Christmas and they were on their way back to France and they couldn't wait to meet up with everyone again. They imagined that Christmas would be a magical time and they weren't disappointed. It was nonstop laughter and happiness for them all and they all agreed that it had been the best Christmas that they could remember, even though they missed having Lauren and Samuel with them. But they had to accept that they were adults now and had their own lives to live with other things to do. They didn't however, have no contact with their young ones because they both telephoned to wish their parents Seasons Greetings and told them that they loved and missed them all. All too quickly the festivities were over and during the lull between Christmas and New Year the friends were able to discuss the work on offer fully and to finalise arrangements for the forthcoming move.

It was a rather sombre David who waited for an opportunity to talk to Richard on his own and then he confided in Richard that he was beginning to get worried about Marion. He told him that he had noticed her on occasion holding her head in her hands and she would occasionally lose her balance for no apparent reason. When he approached her about it she dismissed his worries as nothing for him to bother about. He told Richard that his wife wanted this move more than anything and he didn't want his concerns to get in the way of her happiness. He also asked Richard not to say anything about his concerns to Marion just in case he was reading too much into what he had seen. Richard agreed, he patted David on the shoulder and told him not to worry and said that he was probably becoming over protective. The two men then shook hands and went to find themselves a nice cold beer to relax with.

New Years Eve arrived and the farmhouse was filled with happy smiling faces as the estate workers, their wives and partners celebrated with their employers. It was a wonderful night, one for all of them to remember with music singing and dancing. They were all having so much fun that no-one noticed Marion slip away from the party. Her head was throbbing again and she needed to lie down and rest in the peace and quiet of their room. She told herself that she would be alright after a short sleep and that she only needed to get away from the noise for a short space of time. A little later David realised that his wife was missing from the festivities and went to look for her. He found her asleep on the top of their bed and he gently lowered himself down to sit beside her. Then he gazed at the woman he loved so much and thought how beautiful she looked with her now greying hair slightly tousled and falling over her face. The laughter lines around her mouth and eyes appeared to be heightened by the pallor in her skin. As he sat there he sent out a silent prayer for his love to be made fit and well again because he was sure, within his own mind that her condition had returned, although he would never suggest as much to her.

New Year's morning arrived and the friends were amazingly up bright and early. They all agreed that the previous evening had been a huge success for them and their workers and now it was back to business. After lunch David and Marion packed their suitcase into the boot of their car ready to begin the journey back home where they would begin preparations for their new life in France. David noticed that Marion was unusually quiet as they journeyed home and he hoped that it was due to the excitement of the night before. He breathed a sigh of relief as they pulled up onto their own driveway. He got out of the car, helped Marion out and then supported her as they walked into the house together. David settled her onto the sofa and went into the kitchen to make them both a much needed cup of tea. He hummed a tune as he carried the two tea cups into the lounge placing Marion's on the small table at the side of the sofa. She was asleep so he drank his tea and then fetched the suitcase in from the boot of the car. He decided not to disturb his wife for an hour or so, he would let her sleep while he found one or two little jobs to do in the garden but before he went he lit the gas fire to keep her warm.

He put the terracotta pots into his shed to protect them from the frost, swept a few leaves up and then went into the house. It was far too cold to stay out there any longer he told himself. He called to Marion from the kitchen and asked her if she wanted a fresh cup of tea but he still got no reply from her. He decided to leave her another half an hour and then he would have to wake her up or she wouldn't sleep at bedtime. Half an hour later and he gently took his wife by the shoulders and gave her a shake. "Wake up sleepy head," he joked as he shook her again. As he shook her, her lifeless head rolled forward and he knew that his greatest nightmare had been realised. He sank down into the seat beside her and cradled her in his arms. Time seemed to stand still as he held her close to him. in a daze he got up and then placed her lifeless body full length along the sofa. He eventually made the necessary phone calls and sat and waited for the doctor and ambulance to arrive. When the formalities were completed and every one had gone his first thought was to ring Samuel on his mobile. He prayed that his son would hear the call and answer. He needed to hear the familiar sound of his voice but he needn't have worried because Samuel picked up almost immediately. He could hear his son's cheery voice asking him what was wrong because it was always his mother who spoke to him first when he got a call from home.

The phone was silent for a moment as David tried to compose himself before he spoke. A moment later he was able to tell his son about his mothers' sudden passing. Samuel was suddenly struck dumb by the news but eventually he was able to tell his father that he would be with him tomorrow because he was on the way back home with some news of his own. It was a very quiet and withdrawn young man who made the journey home to see his father. How he wished that Lauren was going to be there as she had been all of his life. The next phone call David had to make was to his friends in France they needed to know as soon as possible because now, life could never be the way that they had planned for each other.

The following day there was a knock on the door and when he answered it Claire stood before him her eyes brimming with tears. She followed him into the house and they clung together in their grief at Marion's death. He told her that he had been suspicious of his wife's condition for a few weeks but she had always insisted that there was nothing wrong and he should stop worrying. Claire confessed to him that she and Richard had been aware of something being wrong with her over the Christmas period. They had, she said observed that Marion had lost her sparkle and the spring in her step which had always been indicative of her friend. Claire went into David's kitchen and put the kettle on for a strong, hot, sweet cup of tea because she for one needed it. David agreed, followed her and sat at the kitchen table which is where Samuel found them about half an hour later. His father jumped up from the table and hugged him as if never to let him go.

"I have never been so pleased to see anyone," he told Samuel when he finally released him from his grip. He told his son to sit down while Claire poured him a drink and then he told him about the events of the day before. She walked out of the kitchen and into the lounge. She didn't want to intrude on father and son as they were drawn even closer by their shared grief. When the two men joined her in the lounge they both told her that she shouldn't have left them alone. She was the closest thing to family to both of them and she must never feel otherwise. She hugged each of them in turn with tears slowly running down her face and told them that she had always considered them to be part of her family too. When David finally closed his eyes and drifted into a troubled sleep Claire told Samuel that if it would help his father she was willing to go with him to get the death certificate and anything else which they may require. But she told him that although she would be with them for moral support the actual funeral arrangements she would leave to him and his father. Samuel thanked her and said that he would be grateful for any support that she could give him at the moment.

Later that evening she excused herself and said that she wanted to ring Lauren and tell her what had happened. She went to the spare guest room where she could talk to Lauren freely without causing any more upset for two men down stairs. She finally got hold of her daughter on the third time of trying. Lauren apologised to her mother when she told her how long she had been trying to get her. She told her mother that she had only just got back to her room where she had left her mobile. That was fine her mother assured her and then told her to sit down because she had some bad news to tell her. Lauren sat in disbelief as her mother explained what had happened. She felt shell shocked because she hadn't known about the tumour which Marion had suffered with the previous year. Her mother said that Samuel hadn't wanted to worry her unnecessarily and especially as his mother appeared to have beaten the condition. Lauren thanked her mother for informing her and said that she would contact Samuel the following day. She also said that it would be very doubtful that she could attend the funeral as they had just begun an important dig in Egypt. Her mother told her not to trouble herself about it and she would tell Samuel to expect her call the next day. Before the conversation ended Lauren told her mother how much she loved her and her father and said that she missed them very much although she was enjoying her life doing the things that she had always wanted to do. Her mother said that she understood and that she and her father loved her more than anything else in the world.

The following two weeks were the worst that Claire could remember. David had withdrawn into himself and both she and Samuel found it very difficult to reach him. He showed no interest in anything and wouldn't even help Samuel sort out the funeral arrangements. He was so glad that he could lean on Claire and bounce his ideas off her. He needed his father but at the moment he felt quite isolated from him, he felt that he had to take the responsibility of everything on his own shoulders.

On the morning of the funeral Marion was taken into the tiny church where she and Claire had first become friends so many years ago. The weight of so many memories hung heavy on her heart as she followed David and Samuel behind the coffin and then sat with them at the front of the church. The vicar was a kind sensitive man who performed the service with great feeling and understanding. He had come to know both women very well over the years as he often chatted with them when they visited their children's graves. He knew of the deep seated pain which both women carried deep within their hearts.

When the service was over her coffin was carried to the plot of ground which she and David had reserved for them many years ago, so that, when the time came they could be buried next to their precious baby girls. At last it was time to leave the Cemetery and make their way home to that empty house which held so many memories and which David was having trouble coping with. He confided in Claire that he couldn't see a way forward. He didn't know how he could carry on with his life without his darling Marion at his side. She had always been his strength. He was nothing without her.

Claire spoke to Richard the following day and said that she would be staying with David for another two weeks. Samuel had to go back to College at the end of the week. He had already been absent from College without permission and he needed to explain his actions to the Principal when he returned. He hoped with every fibre of his body that his place was still secure on the course.

Chapter 31

S amuel had returned to College and Claire was doing her best to help David cope but they both knew that there was only so much that she could do. He had got to learn to face the future alone now he needed to draw on his own inner strength. So it came as a shock to Claire when David announced that he had decided to go into a Care Home. He knew of the time which Claire had spent working in a home quite close to where they lived and he asked her to go with him to find out the availability of a room there. She could see the sense in his decision and agreed to accompany him there. She understood that he could make a new life for himself without all of the reminders around him in his own home but she also realised that that in the home he wouldn't feel isolated. He would still be quite close to Marion's resting place and he could visit whenever he wanted. He rang the Care Home and made an appointment to view it the following afternoon. They did have a vacancy and if it suited it could be his for the taking.

The following afternoon Claire stood with a slightly anxious David in the middle of a light, airy room at the Home. Matron stood with them and asked them what they thought of it. She pointed out that there was room enough for David to bring some of his personal furniture should he wish. She suggested that perhaps he might have a favourite chair that he might like to bring. There was always the possibility of bringing a small chest of drawers and the bare walls would benefit from having a few pictures or photographs hanging on them. David sat on the edge of the single bed which stood alongside the far wall in the room. He looked at Claire and said that he thought he could be very happy in this place particularly if he had his most precious belongings with him. Matron then asked David if he would like to see the rest of the amenities which the Home had to offer. She said that it would give her a chance to introduce him to the other residents. She asked Claire to find a seat and make herself comfortable while she took David into her office to discuss details. Claire sat in the residents' lounge along with a few of the residents. They had a short conversation about the weather and other mundane matters and then most of the residents had an afternoon nap.

Claire sat in the silence for a short while and then her mind wandered back to the happy times she had spent working there with her special residents. The piano still stood in the corner of the room and as she closed her eyes she could visualise William and Helena at their Thursday afternoon sing along times. The thought of them brought a smile to her face and the realisation that she hadn't thought about them or this place for years. The thought of forgetting two people who had brought joy into the lives of others made her rather sad and she silently promised herself that she would never forget them again. She was jolted back to the present by the sound of conversation behind her. She turned her head towards the direction of the voices and saw David shaking hands with Matron and he looked happier than she had seen him for days. Matron disappeared towards her office and then she and David made their way to the outside door. He told her that he had agreed to take the room as soon as he could. He thought that he might be looking at a time scale of about a month because he wanted to empty the house and then put it on the market. He had decided to get a house clearance firm in to take the furnishings that he didn't want to take with him. Then he told her he would put the house up for sale. The final thing he wanted to do was to update his will he didn't want his son to have any legal problems when it was his time to go he told her.

At last Claire felt happy to go home and leave him to complete his plans so she told him that she would be going back to France at the end of the week. Richard took one of her hands and held it between both of his. She could feel the love and gratitude flowing from him as he thanked her for being the best friend that anyone could wish for. Without her strength he couldn't have faced the future he told her and he leaned toward her and carefully placed a gentle kiss on her cheek. She told him that she had only done what any good friend would have done but she was pleased to know that she had made a difference for him. The next day was a busy one with Claire helping him to sort through what he wanted and what he was going to dispose of. She was relieved to see him taking charge of his life again and now couldn't wait for the following day to arrive so that she could make her way back to her husband and her own life which she had missed so much.

As he waved her off David promised that he would be in touch as soon as he was settled into his new home also, that he had decided to write to Samuel to keep him up to date with all the changes. He thought that a letter was the best way to tell his son because he would have all the information in black and white. He thought that Samuel might forget some of the important information if he told him over the phone and besides which he could express himself better in a letter.

When Claire arrived back at the farmhouse she kicked her shoes off put the kettle on and then sank into her favourite armchair situated at the side of the large range fire. I could sleep for a week she laughed as both Wendy and Richard asked how everything had gone with David. She looked at Richard and asked him to make the coffee and then she recalled everything which had happened. Richard put his arms around her and said that he knew that if anyone could help David it was her. He told her how very proud he was of her. She only smiled at him and took the compliment with the grace with which it was given.

Slowly their lives drifted into a routine revolving around the early mornings and the late evenings but this time there was a big difference. Wendy had employed the wife of one of the vineyard workers as a housekeeper. There were no more nights of not knowing what to have to eat because they were all too tired to cook. Now, the table was always set for their meal and the most appetising smells met them at the door. They all agreed that Madame Duval was the most important asset they had. As time went by their business began to flourish and grow at a rate that was far beyond their expectations. They were all kept so busy that the thoughts of David drifted further and further away until one day when the telephone rang and Richard heard his voice on the other end. He said that he had been thinking a lot about them lately and if possible he would like to arrange a visit with them. He had gotten permission from the Matron and he could have a carer come with him. He said that she was a lovely girl and she would take care of his needs while they were there. She was due her summer holiday break in two weeks and he wondered whether that would be convenient for them. Richard was thrilled at the news and said that they would all be delighted to see him again and have the chance to catch up with all of his news. He said that they would make two of the old holiday lettings available for them. They only needed a bit of a face lift and that would be no problem. They always had someone there who was looking for work so that could soon be arranged. Richard told him that they would expect to see him in two weeks but if there was a change of plan he only had to ring and tell them.

In their small amount of spare lime Claire and Wendy busied themselves changing curtains and renewing the bed linen for the holiday let's while Madame Duval's two burly sons cleaned and decorated the two buildings. By the end of the week, the rooms looked neat, tidy and clean. "All the rooms will need next week before they arrive will be a couple of vases of flowers just to give them a homely feel." Wendy said as she thought out loud. "I couldn't agree with you more." Claire said chuckling to herself.

Although Claire was anxious to see David she couldn't help but wonder. Why should he need a carer because the last time she saw he was managing very well for himself? The answer was very apparent the following week when David arrived being pushed in a wheel chair by a young woman who introduced herself as Sarah. Wendy showed them to their rooms and left them to settle in before they all got together that evening. She told Claire later that she was glad that they had decided to house them in the holiday accommodation because they would have had difficulty trying to get David in to the farmhouse up all of those steps. As the evening began the atmosphere was a slightly strained and awkward as the friends were all missing Marion being among them. It didn't feel right without her there but David soon eased the tension by telling them that he had come to terms with what had happened and beside which Marion wouldn't want them to be sad about her passing. She had enjoyed her life and she would expect them to carry on in the same manner as they always had.

"As for me," he said as he patted the side of the wheel chair. "I had another stroke shortly after I moved into the home and as you can see I am not as mobile as I was." He went on to say that he thought that this would be the last time that he could make the journey to see them so he was going to make the most of this opportunity. He also told them that he had taken up water colour painting with Sarah's help. She had started a painting class at the Home for all of the residents to enjoy and he was taking full advantage of it. He told them that while they were there he and Sarah would be spending a lot of time in the nearby countryside because he loved painting landscapes and this was a perfect location. He explained that they didn't need to make any special arrangements for him because he and Sarah would be fine. He didn't want to interrupt their busy working days. He was just so happy to be here with them for the next two weeks.

One evening as the friends sat talking and simply enjoying each other's company Claire asked David about what had happened to Samuel when he had gone to Africa to visit Joanne. She said that when she saw him last she hadn't had time to ask him but she could see that something was wrong. David admitted that his heart had gone out to his son when he explained the outcome of that visit. Samuel, he said was very taken with Joanne and was hoping that they had a future together when all of their commitments were filled but when he saw her all of his hopes were shattered. His son had told him that when he saw Joanne it was the biggest shock of his life. The woman who had approached him didn't look like Joanne. She wore the white robes of a postulate nun and walked with a grace and calmness which he wouldn't ever have associated with her. She told him that from the moment she had arrived at the school she had the sense that her life would change and that she would never be the same person again. She told him the more time she spent among the nun's the more she wanted be a part of their way of life. She had only been at the school six months when she spoke to the Mother Superior and told her of her wish to join the convent. She was told by the Mother Superior that it was a decision not to be taken lightly and to go away and think about it. After a few months she had shown that she was ideally suited to the life so Mother Superior relented and welcomed her into their way of life as a postulate. Joanne had told him that she had never been happier and that she had found her calling. Samuel was devastated but he bowed to her wishes and wished her well in her new life. David told Claire that Samuel had then decided to travel for a few months and that was why he was so late going back to College. Claire asked him what Samuel was doing now and he told her that since he qualified Samuel had gone to India and was working in a Sanctuary for his favourite animals the Bengal Tigers. Claire could hardly believe the information which David had just given her but she said that she hoped Samuel was happy and keeping well.

Time flew by and soon it was time for David to return home but before he left he gave them a painting of the farmhouse and vineyard as a thank you and as a memento of his time with them. They were all delighted and amazed by the gift and they all agreed that he showed an exceptional talent. "It will take pride of place over the fire place in the lounge," Wendy told him touching him warmly on the arm as he wheeled himself toward the door where Sarah stood waiting for him. The three friends stood side by side as they waved a tearful goodbye to David and they all felt as though it was probably the last time that they would see him. Life they agreed was very strange indeed and now they needed to carry on with theirs. Business had taken an upward surge and now they were contemplating getting a manager in. The workload was becoming too much for any of them to have some quality time of their own and they had to agree that none of them were getting any younger. Wendy was particularly feeling the strain and remarked in passing one day that she was looking forward to the day she could retire. She reminded them that it had now been six years since they purchased the winery and while she had loved every minute of it she felt that it was now time for her to slow down a little and take it easy. Both Claire and Richard understood what she was saying and also if she wanted to slowly take less responsibility and take a back seat from the business they would do all that they could to help her achieve her goal. Richard confided in Claire one evening when they were sitting alone on the porch that he wished that Samuel and Lauren were closer to take over and take control of everything. Claire agreed that it would be the ideal solution but unfortunately their offspring were too busy living their own lives. For which she didn't blame them. It was after all their dream to live this life not their children's. "Talking of which," she said. "I had a letter from Lauren this morning and it sounds as if she will be coming home for a visit shortly." Richard was delighted, he couldn't remember the last time he had seen his daughter. She had kept regular contact with her parents over the years but that wasn't the same as her physical presence. He said that he couldn't wait and his face lit up at the thought of her being there with them.

Chapter 32

It was a balmy autumn evening when they heard a familiar voice calling out, "Mom, Dad, where are you?"

"Lauren!" they shouted in unison as they dashed out of the bottling plant in the direction of their daughter's voice. Five minutes later and the three of them stood hugging each other amidst a flood of tears and laughter. They had waited far too long for this moment and no-one wanted to break the spell of the minute. They parted at last and with arms draped around each other they walked towards the farmhouse where Wendy stood with open arms ready to welcome Lauren home in her own inimitable way.

"My, how well you look," said her mother as she stood beside her daughter who was glowing with health and happiness.

"Come, sit at the table while I lay another place," said Wendy as she beckoned to the empty chair.

"Madame Duval always leaves us a generous amount of delicious food so I am sure there will be more than enough for the four of us." she assured Lauren as she questioned whether there would be enough for all four of them.

"Mmm! Lovely," said Lauren as the aroma of coq-au- vin filled the kitchen as Wendy opened the range door.

"I can't remember the last time I enjoyed a meal so much." said Lauren as she ate the last bit of a crusty batten. She looked at her mother with a cheeky grin and said. "It was better than your cooking mother." They all had to laugh because Claire had never been the best cook in the world. After the meal Wendy told them to go and sit in the lounge she would deal with the washing up tonight. "You go and have some family time." she told them. "It will be good for you all to catch up without me in the way."

Claire told her not to be so silly they were all family together but Wendy said "No," this was their time. She gently touched Wendy on the arm by way of a thank you and Wendy nodded to say she understood. Claire and Richard had so many questions for their daughter but above all they wanted to know what had made her decide to come back home now? She told her parents that in some way it was a form of escapism. She had been so happy with Ian travelling the world exploring so many different dig sites. She had seen some of the most beautiful places on earth and she had learned so much working with such an informed individual. They had become very close over the years and she thought that they could be very happy together she told them. She could, at times imagine being married to him and having a family but every time he had proposed she had found some reason to say "No." She couldn't explain the logic behind her answers she confessed but each time he asked there was something inside which was saying "No." She loved him dearly she said but it wasn't enough for her to give in to her feelings and say "Yes," to him.

He had she confessed proposed in some of the romantic places imaginable. The first time they were travelling up the Nile on a river cruise when he popped the question. Another time he had taken her to Venice but she still couldn't say "Yes." The last time she refused him they were at Victoria Falls. She told them that as she refused him she wasn't sure whether he was shedding tears or whether it was the spray from the falls. Either way, they decided there and then that their situation couldn't continue and they agreed to go their separate ways. She broke down in tears as she told her mother of the huge gap which it had left in her life but in the long term it could never have worked. She couldn't explain the feeling that she had inside that there was someone out there who she was destined to be with and she just hadn't met him yet.

Her mother did her best to comfort her and then changed the subject by asking about the places she had seen and the digs she had been involved with. Wendy joined them later and they all enjoyed a glass of wine before retiring to their beds. When they were alone Richard said that he knew what she had been thinking while Lauren was speaking about Ian. He said that he had always thought himself that Lauren and Samuel belonged together. Perhaps it would have been easier if they had been brought up as strangers and met, rather than always thinking of one another as an extension of their own family. I know what you mean she told her husband but it's too late to think about it now. Tomorrow is another day and we still have to find out if Lauren has any plans for the future. I would like to think that she had come home to stay said Claire as she nestled into the comfortable warmth of her husband as he lay beside her.

Lauren awoke at first light and lay in bed listening to birds singing their dawn chorus. That was one of the things she had missed during her travels but it was only now that she realised how much. She lay enjoying the sound for a short while and then she arose and went into the kitchen to cook them all a real English breakfast. Her parents and Wendy awoke to the aroma of bacon and sausages wafting up the stairs.

"That smells good," said Richard as he raced past his wife and hurried down stairs.

"We don't usually have a full English breakfast," he said as he took his place at the table.

"We normally have a light meal in the morning but I must admit I am starving and I can't wail to get my teeth into it."

They all laughed at him and then sat in silence to eat their own meals. With breakfast over and the washing up done and the pots put away before Madame Duval arrived Claire asked her daughter if she had any plans for the day. Lauren said that she hadn't and she would like to spend the day wandering around and just getting the feel of the place. Her parents said that would be fine but if she got bored they could always find her a job to do in the winery. Lauren agreed, put on a jacket and set off to explore the places that she and Samuel had played in as a child. She had always felt such a sense of freedom in this place and she was surprised that it had not disappeared with time. She could close her eyes and almost imagine that she was a child again. It was a wonderful morning but the feeling was spoiled because she was alone. Then almost like a flash of light she was struck by the realisation that it was Samuel she wanted not as a brother figure but as a part of her. She new for the first time in her life, that they belonged together. They were like two sides of the coin. She could never be truly happy until he was at her side as her husband. She sat down and leaned against an olive tree which stood some distance away from the farmhouse and cried. She felt a sudden rush of anger mixed with despair at the thought that he may never know how she felt. She didn't even know where he was in the world or what he was doing. The thought, that there was the possibility that he might even be married struck terror in her heart.

The wind began to cool as she sat on the ground leaning against the tree. She pulled her jacket close around her and decided to make her way back to the farmhouse and to the people she loved. She felt that she could never tell them her thoughts so she tried to bury her feelings inside and made up her mind that without Samuel she would never marry anyone. She would spend the rest of her life alone.

She told her parents that she had made the decision to stay and that she wanted to become part of the business. She wanted to ease herself in gently, working her way up from the bottom. She was determined to know the business inside out before she could think of taking any position of responsibility. Her parents and Wendy were overjoyed at her decision and promised to do all in their power to help her. She was true to her word and twelve months later Wendy was able to hand over her part of the business to Lauren. She informed them all that she wished to call an executive meeting as soon as possible as there was something very important she wished to discuss with them. They arranged a meeting for the following Friday. They were all curious as to what was on the agenda but Wendy said that she had to finalise some details before she could tell them anything. They were all curious about what was so important and what was Wendy doing? But they all resigned themselves to the fact that they would have to wait until Friday.

The time of the meeting finally arrived and they all sat silently waiting for Wendy to begin her explanation. They didn't have to wait long as Wendy addressed them almost immediately. She apologised for making them wait so long for an explanation but there had been something she needed finalise before she could speak to them. They all sat listening intently as she continued. She told them that she had been wanting to retire for a couple of years and now that Lauren had taken to the business so well she felt that now would be the ideal opportunity. She had, she informed them finalised the purchase of a small cottage approximately five miles away on the previous day. It would be far enough away for her to live a quiet life now although it would still be close enough for daily contact if that was what they wanted. She also told them that she wanted to transfer her shares in the business to Lauren. They all sat in stunned silence for a moment or two no-one was sure what to say. Eventually, Richard said that if that was what she truly wanted then of course they were all in agreement. She also told them that she had transferred ownership of the farmhouse to him and Claire, she would be quite happy in her new little cottage where she could spend time tending the small garden which surrounded it. Richard asked when was she thinking of moving and she said almost immediately. The cottage was in pristine condition and all she had to do was move her things in. They agreed to discuss the situation more informally later after they had all had time to have a cup of tea and think about the future outcome of the decision which they had just made. Wendy closed the meeting and made their way into the farmhouse and the hot welcome cup of tea which they would soon be enjoying.

Two weeks later saw Wendy sitting in her own small lounge with nothing but the sound of silence around her. She knew that it would take some getting used to but it was what she needed now. She had loved ever} minute of living in the farmhouse and all of the challenges which it had thrown at her but now she was tired and needed the peace and time to do the things that she wanted to do. The business had provided her with a comfortable retirement which she was determined to take full advantage of while she still had the health and strength to do so. She had the time now to ponder on the past and her thoughts wandered to David and the day that they received that dreadful telephone call telling them that he had suddenly been taken ill and had passed into the Spirit World. She recalled that it had happened only three months after his last holiday with them. Sarah had been heartbroken as she relayed the details to Claire. Wendy remembered the day that they went to his funeral service, which he had organised himself, leaving detailed instructions so no-one had to worry about anything. She also remembered the immense feeling of sadness that neither, Samuel, or Lauren was able to attend the service as they were both in some far corner of the world and couldn't reach home in time. She smiled to herself as she admired David's forethought in covering every minute detail of his wishes for exactly that sequence of events. She gently sighed as she thought of the hole that his passing had left in their lives and how relieved she was that Lauren was finally home. If only Samuel could be with her then life would be perfect she mused.

Chapter 33

Wendy settled into retirement happily with the occasional visit to the farmhouse to see her friends. The business was prospering with Lauren taking on more and more of the running of the winery leaving Monsieur Le Claire to take complete control of managing the vineyard. Richard and Claire were happy to relinquish the running of the business to their daughter. It was, a wish come true for her happy parents. They had. since going into partnership with Wendy hoped that Lauren would one day want to settle down in France and take over their responsibilities. They did. however, both agree that in an ideal world Samuel would be at Lauren's side because they had always known that the two of them belonged together. It was a fact, which neither of their children appeared to have accepted. Although Claire had her suspicions that Lauren had lately been thinking along the same lines as her. She had seen the wistful look in her daughter's eyes. It was a look she knew only too well, she had seen it so often over the years when Lauren had been remembering the happy times that she had spent with Samuel as they were growing up.

Claire and Richard monitored their daughter's progress from a distance for the following twelve months and they both agreed that she had become quite a discerning business woman. So much so that they could now take the retirement that was long due to them. They had been discussing the possibility between themselves for a long period of time and now they felt that it was the right time to tell Lauren. There was nothing more that they could teach her. She had earned the right through shear hard work to become sole owner of the business and they couldn't be happier. As they sat around the dining table that evening Lauren's parents told her of their plans. She was taken aback at first. She had realised that they had taken a back seat for a while but she hadn't realised that they were seriously considering retirement. But her father assured her that it was what he and her mother needed now. They had both past retirement age and like Wendy they now needed to live out their days in peace and relaxation. They told her that they wanted to move closer to the coast. The thought of evening strolls along the beach was very appealing to them both. They also pointed out that it would be somewhere for her to visit whenever she felt like getting away for a few days. She assured them that she thought it was a wonderful idea although she felt a little overawed taking on full responsibility of running everything herself. Her father smiled at her, put his arm around her shoulder and told her that she was perfectly capable of making an even bigger success of the business than they had. Besides which, he and her mother assured her she could always rely on their help if she needed it, although they were positive that she wouldn't need their help. They were so proud of their daughter their hearts were fit to burst.

They began their search for a new home almost immediately. Over the next six months they viewed 40 properties and none of them promised to give them what they were looking for. Claire confessed to Richard one evening that she didn't think that they were going to find the right place and that she was thinking that they should move back to England. Richard held her in his arms and said that if they didn't find something soon that they would sit down and have a discussion about their options. He told her that he didn't want to give up looking just yet as he had a feeling that they would find exactly what they were looking for even if they weren't sure what that was at the moment. They agreed on a time scale of another month and if they still hadn't found their new home they would consider the alternative option of returning home to England.

Two weeks later they came across a small fishing village on the south coast. The location was exactly what they were looking for although the cottages were all occupied and none of them were on the market. They despondently walked down onto the beach, kicked their shoes off and walked slowly along it taking in the sights as they went. The tiny fishermen's cottages sat in a semi-circle around the beach. How pretty they looked in the sunshine with flower filled baskets hanging from every wall and window boxes beneath almost every window. The cottage fronts stood against the very narrow footpath so none of them had a front garden but the occupants more than made up for the fact with the colourful displays on the walls of their cottages. People seemed to be everywhere chattering and laughing amongst themselves. What a happy place this appeared to be. This was exactly what they had been looking for.

They stood in silence for a while taking in the view before them knowing that this was the kind of place that they had been looking for. Their silence was suddenly broken by a voice calling, "Bonjour Monsieur, bonjour Madame."

They turned to look in the direction of the voice and saw an old man repairing a small rowing boat. He waved to them and they walked towards him. When they reached him Richard replied. "Bonjour Monsieur,"

He gestured to them to sit down beside him while he worked. He asked them what they thought of the village and the surrounding area. They told him that they had both fallen in love with the place and that it was exactly what they were looking for to find their new home. They told him that they were really disappointed that there was nothing on offer there. He looked at them both as though deep in thought for a moment and then a huge smile spread across his old weather beaten face which was full of character. It looked as though it carried a story in every line and wrinkle. Everything about him looked old and wizened, except for his kind pale blue eyes which sparkled with mischief and laughter. During the course of their conversation Claire and Richard told the old man (whose name was Henri) that they had been house hunting for months now but they hadn't been able to find anywhere which felt right until now.

He pointed to a small dirt track which lay just beyond the end cottage. It looked as if it led nowhere but the old man insisted that they go and explore for themselves. They shook his hand and thanked him and, walked towards the entrance to the track. They walked along it for ten minutes and then realised that the scenery was changing around them. The open grassland was turning into woodland with the trees becoming denser the further they walked along the track.

Two hundred metres further on they suddenly stopped and stood staring in amazement at a wood and stone built house nestled in a clearing among the trees. Richard and Claire looked at each other in disbelief. From the outside this house looked perfect. It was everything (hat they could have wished for. They nervously approached the front door to enquire about viewing the property. They rang the bell and were absolutely astonished to see the old man whom they had been talking to on the beach. He laughed at the look of disbelief on their faces and invited them in. He explained that he had ridden on his bicycle along another path to beat them to the house and he then let out another belly laugh.

He showed them into the well appointed kitchen first with its modern units, central isle and huge range oven. Claire was thrilled with the size of the kitchen and couldn't wait to see the rest of the house. He led them into a large sitting room which had an open stone built fireplace with inglenooks either side. It took Claire's breath away as she saw the French doors which led to a sun lounge surrounded by open countryside. Upstairs were two good sized bedrooms and a very modern bathroom. When he had finished showing them the house he took them through a door at the far end of the kitchen, along a short passage and into an annex which had been added on as a fully fitted, one bedroom apartment for his sister but she had passed away before she could live there. Immediately their thoughts went to Wendy. If she wanted to, she could move in with them and then she wouldn't be left alone in her cottage. They could all spend their remaining years together and at the same time be able to live their own separate lives.

When the tour of the house was completed Henri asked them to stay and have a cup of coffee with him when they could discuss the sale of the house further. They were only too pleased to accept his invitation because there were a lot of details to clarify and Claire was curious to know more about this fascinating man. Two and a half hours later saw them waving goodbye to Henri as they began their long walk back along the track towards the main road where they had left their car. The journey home was full of laughter and excitement as they discussed the house, Henri and their new future in this beautiful part of the country.

They called at Wendy's cottage en route but she wasn't there so they continued their journey home to give the good news to Lauren. Their daughter was thrilled for them but at the same time sad because they would be parted again. Since being back at home she had gotten used to having her parents close at hand and she would miss them terribly. However she assured them that if that was where they wanted to be she couldn't be happier for them. They told her that they had called at Wendy's but she was not there and Lauren stifled a giggle as she told them that she had seen Wendy walking past the farmhouse arm in arm with a very distinguished looking gentleman earlier in the day. They couldn't hide their surprise at the news because Wendy had never said a word to them about having a gentleman friend.

Later that evening there was a knock on the kitchen door and a familiar voice calling out to them as they heard the door being opened and then shut again. A glowing Wendy stood before them with her friend standing behind her.

"Find yourselves a seat while I get two more glasses," Richard instructed them.

"It looks as though we have a lot to celebrate this evening," he said, winking at Wendy as he made his way into the kitchen for the glasses.

Wendy's face flushed a little as she introduced her friend when they were all settled a short time later. His name was Thomas and they had past each other on numerous occasions when she had been on one of her long walks through the woods she explained. It was one day when she had been silting painting a particularly pretty wild orchid that Thomas had finally plucked up the courage to speak to her she explained as she turned and smiled at him. He was a retired botanist he had told her and he had been searching the woods for the very flower that she was painting. He told her that it was a particularly rare specimen which he methodically documented while she continued to paint. Wendy told her friends that they had discovered that they had a lot in common and their friendship continued to grow from that day so much so she explained that she was thinking of moving back to England with him. She told them that she loved them all and would miss them terribly but felt that this was the right time for her to make changes in her life and move on.

Claire broke down in floods of tears at the news. She was torn with her emotions because Wendy had been such a great part of her life for so many years. Through the tears she told Wendy that she couldn't be happier for her but at the same time she couldn't be sadder at the thought of losing the company of such a dear friend. The two women hugged and cried together because they were both going through the same mixed emotions. Eventually Claire pulled away and told Wendy that she wished her every happiness and Richard shook Thomas's hand and told him that he had found himself a very special lady in Wendy and he was a very lucky man.

It was almost midnight when Wendy left the farmhouse and her friends behind her. She held tightly onto Thomas's hand as they took their first steps onto another of life's pathways but she knew that this would be the final one for her. The big difference this time was that now she had her own special someone by her side and the thought of him gave her a warm glow inside which she embraced with the whole of her being.

Back at the farmhouse they were left stunned at Wendy's news which had come right out of the blue. They agreed that they were pleased that they hadn't mentioned the house which they had decided to buy whether Wendy had wanted to go with them or not. As they lay in bed encircled in one another's arms a short time later Claire whispered to her husband that she wished that she could see Lauren settled and as happy with someone special. She knew that her daughter was happy in her work but she worried about the lonely hours that Lauren spent at the end of each working day. She sighed and snuggled a little closer to Richard as she accepted the fact that she could do nothing but accept the inevitability of it all. She couldn't remember the last time that they had any form of contact with Samuel and it broke her heart to think that they may never hear from him again. Sleep didn't come easily for her that night as her mind wandered over past memories. So many people had come and gone through her life time. People she had cared for deeply, Annie. David. Marion, William. Helena and of course Wendy. All of these people had brought joy and companionship into her life and each one had their own special place within it.

She thought of her wonderful daughter who had given her and her husband the greatest joy in life. How she wished that Lauren could know the same love in her life that she had found with Richard. She thought of the many times that she had seen Lauren sitting on the top step of the porch, looking across the vineyard. She had seen the sadness in her eyes and she knew that Lauren had been thinking of Samuel, wondering where he was and what he was doing all. Seeing her daughter only confirmed what she had known for years. They belonged together. From the moment they were born there had always been a bond which she could see but which they had so often ignored. Sleep eventually came as she turned her thoughts to the new house and the slower way of life that she and Richard craved and was about to become a reality.

Chapter 34

Samuel awoke to the sounds of the Blue Danube Waltz still swirling around in his head. He could still feel the warmth from her beautiful young body in his arms, her hair like a raven's wing shimmering in the candle light. Why had she suddenly begun disturbing his nights again? As he lay in his bed enclosed by a mosquito net visualising her in his minds' eye. she began to fade. Her hair changed from raven black to the prettiest blonde. Her features began to blur and fade. He opened his eyes and when he closed them again he was not looking at Annie anymore, he was now looking at Lauren. The warmth he had felt in his dream with Annie suddenly multiplied a 1000 fold and in that moment he realised that the girl he had been searching for, for a life time had always been beside him. At last he knew without a shadow of a doubt that Lauren was the girl he needed to share his life with. So many questions race through his mind. How could he have been so blind? What if she didn't feel the same way about him? What if she was married to someone else? He needed to know but where would he begin to find out?

Her parents of course! The idea struck him like a bolt out of the blue. He knew from his Father that they had moved to the farmhouse in France, so he would write to them there. He prayed that they would be able to give him the information which he now craved with every fibre of his being. He realised that his correspondence could take weeks before he had the reply he so badly needed. How could he quell the urgency which had begun to build within him? He resigned himself to trying to be patient although it was very nearly an impossible task. He told himself that he would write the letter that evening but for now he had a pregnant Tiger who urgently needed his professional expertise. She had in the past had a miscarriage and had delivered still born cubs. This time he intended making sure that everything possible would be done to insure that she had a productive labour and delivery. Before he left for the compound he took the calendar off his wall and wrote. "TODAY IS VERY SPECIAL." He replaced the calendar on the wall, got his bag ready to begin his day.

Maya, the tiger was in the last stages of labour when he arrived at her compound and he saw that she was again in great difficulty with the birth. He looked at his colleague, Aroon and told him to get the tranquiliser riffle. He explained that Maya needed a caesarean section now before she lost the cubs again. An hour later and the cubs were delivered safely and they and their mother were returned to the compound. Samuel told Aroon that they should get out quickly as Maya was beginning to awaken and they didn't want to be there when she did. Safely outside Samuel took a deep breath and said that he would make his rounds before taking his break. Aroon told him to stay where he was while he went to reload his rifle with tranquiliser darts. Samuel agreed and was waiting for his colleague's return when he heard a gentle rustle behind him. Thinking that it was Aroon he turned towards the direction of the sound and called out to him. He could see no sign of him although he did catch sight of movement in the grassy undergrowth. He began to walk towards it when he was struck with terror as he caught a glimpse of a pair of golden/yellow eyes watching him. Slowly he began to back up. turned swiftly on his heels and ran like the wind but he couldn't outrun the beast which was now almost upon him. He managed to scream out for help before the animal sprang and knocked him to the ground.

He blacked out as he felt teeth and claws rip through his flesh like a knife through butter. He didn't hear the crack of the hunting rifle as Aroon shot the animal dead. He knew nothing of the horrendous 30 mile journey his colleague made along dusty potholed roads to get him to the hospital where he now lay sedated, unaware of everything going on around him.

It was another two weeks before he was allowed to fully regain consciousness. As he opened his eyes and looked at the nurse attending him her face was blurred by a beautiful mist. Was she an Angel? Had he died and gone to Heaven? His answer came too quickly as the mists disappeared and he felt the agonising pain of her changing the dressings on his back. As his senses returned to him he became aware of not being able to feel or move his legs. Panic began to engulf him. He couldn't stop his mind from imagining all of the worst scenarios he could think of. What if he could never walk again? How could he ever let Lauren know what had become of him? How could she ever be attracted to a cripple? He began to wish that the tiger had killed him. He couldn't face the thought of life without Lauren at his side. He felt himself being dragged down into a pit of overwhelming depression which he had neither, the strength, or the will to climb out of.

The weeks dragged slowly by as the wounds in his back healed but he didn't care. What good was that if he couldn't walk? Mr Patel, the Surgeon had explained to him that when the tiger fell on top of him, its' weight had damaged his spinal cord. He had informed Samuel that there was a slight chance that it could eventually repair itself but it was only a very small chance and that he should prepare himself for the worst. The weeks had turned into months before Samuel was told that he would soon be well enough to be discharged. The impossible was happening and he was at last getting feeling back into his legs and now he couldn't wait to begin to walk again un¬aided. The Physiotherapist had been wonderful with him and Samuel told him that he could never repay him for the precious gift he had given to him. He had given him his life back.

During his stay in hospital Aroon had been his constant visitor. He had brought a smile and encouragement with him whenever he visited and Samuel didn't know what he would have done without his visits to look forward to. They were no longer just colleagues they were friends and the friendship would last a lifetime. This was an unspoken fact which they both acknowledged with brotherly love between them. Aroon had taken his resignation letter to the Sanctuary which Samuel had written whilst recovering. He had also brought Samuel's personal belongings from his room for him and a letter of appreciation from the Sanctuary for all of the dedicated work which he had performed whilst working there.

The two men had often sat and discussed what Samuel's plans would be for when he was discharged from the hospital. He had told

Aroon of the couple he considered his second parents and of course while he talked of Claire and Richard he couldn't help but mention Lauren. Aroon saw the look in his eye whenever he spoke of her and silently prayed to himself that his friend would find the love that he was searching for.

Aroon walked slowly at the side of his friend (who was now walking with the aid of crutches) as the two men made their way out of the hospital towards the car which was waiting to carry them both to the airport and the aeroplane which would carry Samuel to France. Once in France he would ring Claire and Richard to prepare them for his visit. The two men shook hands and then hugged and promised to remain in touch with each other as often as possible. Aroon stood and watched as the plane lifted off the ground and rose high into the sky, taking his friend away from him and carrying him towards a future which he hoped would fulfil his dreams. Samuels' heart beat a little faster with every mile that passed beneath him. Destiny he felt had almost been accomplished. He was heading home.

Finally Samuel found himself walking towards the telephone kiosk in Charles de Gaul Airport, with an old crumpled scrap of paper in his hand with Claire and Richard's number on it. His heart was thumping in his chest as he dialled the number and waited for the receiver at the other end to be lifted. He was speechless for a moment as he heard Lauren's voice at the other end of the telephone. "Hello," "Hello," she repeated before he could bring himself to speak. "Lauren is that really you?" he asked when he was finally able to speak. At the other end of the telephone Lauren was equally shocked to hear Samuel's voice. "Samuel, it's wonderful to hear from you, where are you?" she enquired, as she sat on a chair before her legs buckled beneath her. He explained that he was in the Airport lounge and was hoping to have a few weeks rest with her parents before attempting to find her. She laughed with excitement as she told him to stay where he was and that she would arrange to fetch him herself. She told him to find somewhere to have a meal while he waited, she would be there as soon as she could.

They both replaced the receivers feeling stunned by what they had felt through hearing the sound of each others' voice. Lauren raced into the vineyard to tell Monsieur Le Claire that she would be out for the rest of the day and would he ask Madame Duval to prepare two evening meals? Five minutes later and she was speeding towards the airport. So much love and anticipation racing through her body she didn't know how she was going to contain her feelings when she saw him again. How could she tell him that she loved him and wanted to spend the rest of her life with him? She only knew that somehow she must find a way.

Three hours later a flushed Lauren walked into the Airport lounge. Her eyes scanning and searching everywhere for Samuel, she began to panic, she couldn't see him. Then a familiar voice whispered in her ear, "Do you remember me?" She swung round and was face to face with the man she adored more than anyone in the world. Her arms instinctively swung around his neck but instead of the usual bear hug he gave her, his lips tenderly lowered onto hers in a kiss that promised a life time of love. She melted into his arms as the whole of her body- responded to his touch and in that instant they knew that their destinies had finally been fulfilled.

As Lauren drove them back to the farmhouse she explained to Samuel about her parents' retirement to the coast and that Wendy had moved back to England. She also had so many questions to ask him. She wanted to know about the crutches he was using and why had he left his life in India. He told her that he knew she had a lot of questions and so had he but they had the rest of their lives to satisfy their curiosity. "Tomorrow" he said, "Would be soon enough to start answering questions." "Tonight I want to spend time with you."

When they eventually reached the farmhouse they were giggling like a couple of teenagers again. It felt almost as if time had rolled backwards and the past 15 years had never happened. They felt young again and enthused with a new thirst for life together. They sat and ate their evening meal which Madame Duval had left for them and afterwards Lauren carefully led Samuel out to the porch. It was a warm evening and dusk was slowly descending over the valley as they sat side by side on Lauren's favourite spot on the porch steps. He lovingly placed his arm around her waist as she laid her head on his shoulder. They sat in silence for a few moments drinking in the magical vista before them. Then he cupped her face in his hand and whispered, "I love you."

"I love you too," she replied as his lips lowered onto hers in a kiss filled with an eternity of love, passion and desire. At last the two sides of the same coin could become one. They were where they were destined to be, together.

Chapter 35

E
arly next morning they awoke to the chorus of birdsong and the suns' rays playfully peeping around the half closed curtains. Lauren looked at Samuel as he lay beside her, how she adored him. Her fingers began to idly run through his hair, down the sides of his neck and rested on his muscular shoulders. Her lips soft and full brushed across his as she softly whispered. "Come on sleepy head, we have a lot to do today and it is time that we got started." He lovingly studied her through half closed eye lids, how beautiful she looked with the suns' rays playing on her long blonde hair which cascaded over her shoulders and down her back. He caught her head gently but firmly between his hands and pulled her face towards his. Their lips locked together in a long smouldering kiss. Their bodies moulded together as a life time of love, passion and desire was unleashed and time seemed to stand still as they enjoyed the intimate closeness of each other.

All too soon they were disturbed by the sound of the vineyard and winery coming to life as men's voices rang through the air trying to rise above the noise of machinery and running engines. They finally got out of bed, showered and dressed before going downstairs and into the kitchen where Madame Duval was preparing breakfast. Lauren introduced her to Samuel and told her that he would be living there from now on. They enjoyed a leisurely continental breakfast before they wondered through the vineyard where she introduced him to Monsieur Le Claire and her small army of workers. She informed Monsieur Le Claire that she would be leaving the running of the business in his capable hands for a few days while she and Samuel visited her parents. He was happy to oblige and wished them "Bonne chance!" as they walked away towards the next stage of their journey in life together. But first she must ring her parents to prepare them for their impending arrival.

It was almost lunch time when they arrived at her parents' home. "Wow!" was Samuel's reaction as he stood admiring the house and the beautiful setting surrounding it. Lauren smiled, nodded in agreement and took Samuels' hand as they walked the last few yards towards her parents' front door. They found them in the kitchen preparing a picnic lunch which they were going to eat at the beach. As soon as Claire saw them she dropped what she was doing and gave them both a hug tilled with love and relief that at last all of their wishes had been granted. Their offspring were at last in the kind of relationship which she had always known they were destined for. She and Richard couldn't hide their delight in seeing these two young ones together at last. They all spent two wonderful days together before Lauren told her parents that they would have to return home the following day. Her parents told her that they would be sad to see her leave but, by the same token they were delighted that at last she was happy and in love.

Samuel rose early the next morning and decided to take a walk along the beach before everyone else woke up. He gently kissed Lauren on her forehead, crept out of the room and silently closed the door behind him. When he reached the kitchen he was amazed to see Claire already busy preparing a picnic lunch for him and Lauren to take with them on their journey back home. He told her that he was going for a walk before Lauren woke up and Claire asked him to wait a moment. There was something she wanted to give him without Lauren knowing. He looked at her with a furrowed brow wondering what on earth it could be. She disappeared for a couple of minutes and returned clutching a small black leather box in her hand. Before offering it to him she explained that it was the ring which had belonged to Annie, the girl he had so often dreamed about. She explained that Annie had given it to Richard when he proposed to her. It had been Annie's engagement ring and now it felt right that it should belong to Lauren. She told him that Richard had bought her a diamond ring on their first Wedding Anniversary and that was the ring she had worn every day since. She told him that she had always treasured Annie's ring but now it was time for it to be worn by the person it was always meant for.

She handed the box to Samuel and as he opened it he had the strangest feeling that he knew what Claire meant. It felt to him as though the ring had come home and that it would be worn by the woman he loved so much. He placed it in his pocket and then put his arms around Claire, hugged her and whispered "Thank you Mum." The joy in her heart was overflowing as she gently pushed him away and told him how happy she was to see this day finally arrive. Samuel didn't get his walk along the beach but he got something so much more important and he found it very difficult to conceal his excitement when Lauren finally woke up and joined the family down stairs. An hour later and the two young lovers were back on the road heading toward home. The only stop they made was to eat the picnic lunch which Claire had prepared for them. They were anxious to get home and to start building the rest of their lives together.

As evening began to draw in Samuel and Lauren sat outside on the porch. Lauren had always enjoyed the view- before her but know that Samuel shared it with her it was magical. Samuel arose out of his chair and stood in front of Lauren. He dropped to one knee slowly taking the small black box from his pocket and asked her to be his wife. She gazed at him lovingly and then she looked at the ring nestled in its velvet interior. Her heart skipped a beat as she took the ring and held it in her fingers. She offered it to Samuel and stretched out her left hand towards him. She nodded yes to him as the tears of love and joy filled her eyes and slowly began to drop onto her cheeks. He placed the ring on her finger and kissed it before lifting her out of her chair and taking her into his arms where he knew she was destined to stay for all eternity'.

They began to sway in each others arms to the imaginary sounds of an orchestra playing. They were both transported back in time as the porch suddenly became the magnificent ballroom where Annie and Jamie had promised their love to one another so many decades ago. The simple porch lights became chandeliers hanging along the length of the ceiling and the plain wooden planks became a smooth polished parquet dance floor. They had been transported back to a time of elegance and grace. For a few short moments they too felt like two different people. They realised that although it was they who were dancing, it wasn't themselves that they were looking at. Lauren gazed into the eyes of a handsome young army officer. He looked magnificent in his scarlet tunic with gold braid trim and shiny brass buttons. While he, was holding a beautiful young woman with long black hair, shining like a raven's wing. They could hear the rustle of her midnight blue gown as he swept her along in his arms. Her small, slim body pressed next to his, yielding to his every movement.

All too soon the magic was broken as they heard the telephone ringing but it didn't matter because at last they understood the feelings that had been with them a lifetime and hadn't fully comprehended. Now it was time for Samuel and Lauren. Destiny had finally turned full circle..

The End